Meditations on the Roman Deities

A Guide for the Modern Practitioner

Modern Roman Living Series, Vol. II

L. VITELLIUS TRIARIUS

LVCIVS VITELLIVS TRIARIVS

EX LIBRIS

THIS BOOK BELONGS TO:

_____

Copyright © 2013
L. Vitellius Triarius

All rights reserved.

ISBN-13: 978-1493631780
ISBN-10: 1493631780

Available from Amazon.com, CreateSpace.com, and other retail outlets

www.CreateSpace.com/4504674

Printed by CreateSpace, Charleston SC
An Amazon.com Company

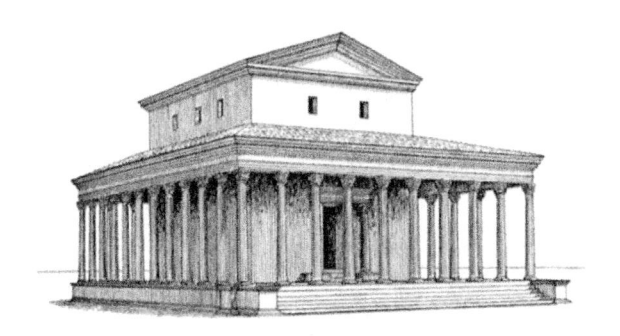

DEDICATIO

Romans, though you're guiltless, you'll still expiate

your fathers' sins, till you've restored the temples,

and the tumbling shrines of all the gods,

and their images, soiled with black smoke.

~Horace, Odes, III, 6

This handbook is dedicated to all those, past, present and future, whose insights into the ancient world of the Romans and personal initiatives have led, are leading, and will lead to an interest in the old ways in the modern age.

LVCIVS VITELLIVS TRIARIVS

CONTENTS

	Acknowledgments	iii
1	Gods and Goddesses of Rome	1
	Dii Consentes	4
	Dii Familiaris	7
	Dii Indigetes	9
	Dii Novensiles	10
	Dii Inferi	10
	The Roman Pantheon	11
2	Prayers to Aesculapius	63
3	Prayers to Apollo	65
4	Prayers to Ceres	74
5	Prayers to Dii Inferi	80
	Faunus	80
	Hecate	80
	Pales	81
	Priapus	82
	Robigo	83
	Terminus	83
6	Prayers to Diana	85
7	Prayers to Hercules	93

8	Prayers to Isis	98
9	Prayers to Janus	104
10	Prayers to Juno	108
11	Prayers to Jupiter	113
12	Prayers to the Lares, Manes et Penates	133
13	Prayers to Magna Deum Mater Idae	141
14	Prayers to Mars	145
15	Prayers to Mercurius	152
16	Prayers to Minerva	156
17	Prayers to Neptunus	159
18	Prayers to Pater Liber	165
19	Prayers to Tellus	170
20	Prayers to Venus	174
21	Prayers to Vesta	180
22	Prayers to Vulcanus	182
23	Prayers I Have Written	183
	About the Author	211

ACKNOWLEDGMENTS

This work is a reference guide of information about the gods and goddesses of Rome for practitioners of the Religio Romana, both for members of Nova Roma, the global Roman Reconstruction effort in our modern age, and those who have not found us yet.

It has been compiled to assist those interested in learning more about the Cultus Deorum Romanum and related Roman culture, both ancient and modern, and has been designed to be of practical use by the religio practitioner and reference guide for the non-practitioner.

Special thanks goes out to the members of the Collegia Pontificum and Augurum, practitioners of the Cultus Deorum Romanum, and Members of the Senate of Nova Roma for their support and assistance in this project.

LVCIVS VITELLIVS TRIARIVS

1 GODS AND GODDESSES OF ROME

Introduction

At the founding of Rome, the gods were numina, divine manifestations, faceless, formless, but no less powerful. The idea of gods as anthropomorphized beings came later, with the influence from Etruscans and Greeks, which had human form. Some of the Roman Gods are at least as old as the founding of Rome.

The concept of numen continued to exist and it was related to any manifestation of the divine. For the Romans, everything in Nature is thought to be inhabited by numina, which explains the big number of deities in the Roman pantheon, as will be shown. Numina manifest the divine will by means of natural phenomena, which the pious Roman constantly seeks to interpret. That's why great attention is paid to omens and portents in every aspect of Roman daily life.

A groups of twelve Gods called Dii Consentes is especially honored by the Romans:

- **Iuppiter**
- **Iuno**
- **Minerva**

- **Vesta**
- **Ceres**
- **Diana**
- **Venus**
- **Mars**
- **Mercurius**
- **Neptunus**
- **Vulcanus**
- **Apollo**

These are the ones listed by the Poet Ennius about the 3rd Century, B.C.E. Their gilt statues stood in the Forum, later apparently in the Porticus Deorum Consentium. As there were six male and six female, they may well have been the twelve worshipped at the lectisternium of 217 BC.

A lectisternium is a banquet of the gods, where the statues of the gods were put upon cushions, and where these statues were offered meals. The number 12 was taken from the Etruscans, which also worshipped a main pantheon of 12 Gods. Nevertheless, the Dii Consentes were not identified with Etruscan deities but rather with the Greek Olympian Gods (though the original character of the Roman Gods was different from the Greek, having no myths traditionally associated). The twelve Dii Consentes are led by the first three, which for the Capitoline Triad. These are the three cornerstones of Roman religion, whose rites were conducted in the Capitoleum Vetus on the Capitoline Hill.

But what better characterizes the traditional Roman Religion is the household or family cult of the Dii Familiaris. In this cult, the Lar Familiaris (guardian spirit - Genius - of the family), the Lares Loci (guardian spirits of the place where the house is built), the Genius of the paterfamilias (House-Father), the Dii Penates (patron gods of the storeroom), the Dii Manes (spirits of the deceased) and a multitude of other domestic deities are daily worshipped by the members of the family. The household cult is so important that it even serves as the model for several practices of the state cult (e.g. there were the Lar Praestites, Penates Publici, etc. Even during the Empire, the Imperial cult came to be based on the household cult, now interpreted as the cult of the Genius of the Emperor, paterfamilias of the family of all the Romans).

Other important Gods are

- **Ianus**
- **Saturnus**
- **Quirinus**
- **Volturnus**
- **Pales**
- **Furrina**
- **Flora**
- **Carmenta**
- **Pomona**
- **Portunus**
- **Fontanus.**

There is also a group of mysterious deities formed by native tutelary deities, river Gods or deified heroes from Latium which are collectively called Dii Indigites (e.g. deified Aeneas, Faunus, Sol Indiges, Iuppiter Indiges, Numicus). A multitude of other deities is also traditionally worshipped, which includes tutelary deities (e.g. Roma, Tiberinus), native Latin deities (e.g. Bellus, Bellona, Liber, Libera), abstract deities such as Fortuna (Fate), Concordia (Concord), Pax (Peace), Iustitia (Justice), etc. Pre-Roman native Italian deities mainly adopted from the Sabines and Etruscans are also worshipped: Nerio (Sabine deity and the consort of Mars), Dius Fidius (Sabine as well), etc. In fact, Quirinus and Vertumnus were also adopted respectively from the Sabines and Etruscans. The Dii Inferi, Gods of the Underworld (Inferus) are Dis/Orcus and Proserpina, equated to the Greek Gods Hades/Plouton (Pluto in Latin) and Persephone. These Gods symbolize the creative power of the Earth which provide human beings the means for subsistence (Dis = wealth = Plouton in Greek). The Inferus is also traditionally regarded as the home for the spirits of the dead, though the concept of afterlife was quite varied.

The pious spirit of the Romans consists of a constant wish to bring the favor of the divine upon him, the family and the state. As such, the Roman is naturally willing to pay the deserved homage and sacrifice to foreign deities, especially if he is in their land. In order to achieve victory in war, the Romans often asked the favor of the Gods of their enemies, paying them sacrifices even greater than those offered by their own people. This spirit joined by the affluence of foreigners which resulted either from trade or conquest, brought new cults to Rome. These were, as expected, democratically adopted by permitting the priests of these Gods to establish temples in Rome. Among the foreign deities, the Dii Novensiles, are Apollo, Ceres (these were adopted as early as to allow them to become part of the Dii Consentes), Bacchus/Dionysus, Sol Invictus Elagabalus, Isis, Serapis, Cybele, Attis, Mithras and many others.

Dii Consentes

Iuppiter is the God of the sky, moon, winds, rain and thunder, who became king of the Gods after overthrowing his father Saturnus. The ancient name of Iuppiter was Diespiter, whose root is Dios (= Zeus, God) + Pater (= Father). As Iuppiter Optimus Maximus, he is the tutelary God of Rome. As a warrior, he is Iuppiter Stator, protector of the City and State who exhorts soldiers to be steadfast in battle. But Iuppiter has many aspects, attributes, names and epithets...

Iuno is Iuppiter's sister, wife and queen of the Gods, is the protectress of the Roman State. Her festival, the Matronalia, is celebrated in March on the Kalends. She is also honored as Iuno Lucetia, celestial light; Iuno Lucina, childbirth, in which the child is brought into light; Iuno Sospita, who protects labor and delivery of children; Iuno Moneta, whose sacred geese warned Rome of an impending invasion. Iuno Moneta's temple was near the mint, thus her name was the root for "money". But Iuno has many aspects, attributes, names and epithets...

Minerva, Goddess of wisdom and learning, meditation, inventiveness, accomplishments, the arts, spinning and weaving, and commerce. Minerva was identified with Pallas Athene, bestower of victory, when Pompey the Great built her temple with the proceeds from his eastern campaigns. Minerva and Mars are honored Quinquatras, five days at the Spring equinox. But Minerva has many aspects, attributes, names and epithets...

Vesta is the Goddess of hearth and home, of domestic and religious fire. Her festival is the Vestalia, held on June 7, when Her temple is open to all mothers who bring plates of food. Vesta's temple was the hearth of Rome, where the sacred fire burned. The fire was tended by six Vestal Virgins, priestesses who were dedicated to the Goddess' service for thirty years, and who were headed by the Virgo Maxima, the eldest Vestal. Vestals were always preceded by lictors, the only women in Rome allowed the privilege. If a condemned man met a Vestal, he was reprieved. When a Roman made his will, he entrusted it to the Vestal Virgins. But Vesta has many aspects, attributes, names and epithets...

Ceres is the Goddess of agriculture. During a drought in 496 BCE, the Sibylline Books ordered the institution of the worship of Demeter, Dionysus and Persephone, called by the Latin names Ceres, Liber and Libera. Ceres was the Goddess of the plebeians: the Ædiles Plebis cared for her temple and had their official residences in it, and were responsible for the games at the Cerealia, her original festival on April 12-19. There was a women's 9-day fast and festival when women offered the first corn harvest to Ceres, originally celebrated every five years, but later - by the time of Augustus - held every October 4.

Diana, Goddess of the Moon and of wild places, the Divine Huntress, protectress of women and virgin Goddess. In earlier times, She was the mother Goddess of Nature. Her temple at Lake Nemi was in a sacred grove and was guarded by her priest, the Rex Nemorensis, the King of the Wood. He was always an escaped slave who was entitled to food, sanctuary and honor - until he was slain by the next candidate. But Diana has many aspects, attributes, names and epithets...

Venus was originally a Goddess of Spring, flowers and vines. By order of the Sibylline Books a temple on Mt. Eryx was dedicated to Venus as the Goddess of love and beauty. She was also Venus

Genetrix, mother of the Roman people through Her son Aeneas, Who was also an ancestor of the Julii. Both Julius Caesar and Hadrian dedicated temples to Venus Genetrix. Hadrian's still stands near the Flavian Amphitheatre. She has darker aspects too, such as Venus Libitina, an aspect of Venus associated with the extinction of life force. But Venus has many aspects, attributes, names and epithets...

Mars, God of war, was originally an agricultural God whose character changed with that of His people. For this reason, he is the most Roman of the Gods, representing the abundance of the fields, and the battles that must be won to keep and enlarge the provinces that kept Rome fed and thriving. His priests were dancing warriors, the Salii, who sang their war-songs in the streets during his festivals. His sacred spears and 12 shields were kept in his temple on the Palatine Hill. But Mars has many aspects, attributes, names and epithets...

Mercurius is the God of commerce. The guild of merchants honored Mercurius at his temple near the Circus Maximus on his festival on May 15. They also sprinkled themselves and their merchandise with sacred water in a ceremony at the Capena Gate. When Mercurius became identified with Hermes, he took on the duties of messenger of the Gods, Psychopompus who guides the souls of the dead through the Underworld, and God of sleep and dreams. He also became God of thieves and trickery, owing to a trick he had played on Apollo by stealing and hiding the Sun God's cattle. His serpent-twined staff, the caduceus, was originally a magician's wand for wealth (which may be why it is the symbol of the medical profession) but became identified later as a herald's staff. But Mercurius has many aspects, attributes, names and epithets...

Neptunus, God of all the fresh water (from rivers, springs, etc.) and of equestrian accomplishments. Equated to the Greek Poseidon, He is also the God of the sea. He had temples in the Circus Flaminius and later on the Campus Martius. His festival, the Neptunalia is celebrated on July 23. But Neptunus has many aspects, attributes, names and epithets...

Vulcanus, the God of the fire of the sky, the lightning and the fires caused by it, he is the raging fire (opposed to the domestic fire, Vesta). He was equated to the Greek Haephestus, God of the fire, forge and volcanos. As a Nature God, he was married to Maia, Goddess of Spring. Equated to Haephestus, he made Iuppiter's thunderbolts and married to Venus. At his festival, the Volcanalia on August 23, fishes were thrown into the hearth fires. The eruption of mount Vesuvius in 79 AD took place in the day of His festival. As God of metal workers, He also has a festival on May 23. As God of conflagration, His temples were built outside the pomerium, on the Campus Martius. But Vulcanus has many aspects, attributes, names and epithets...

Apollo, Greek God of the Sun, prophecy, archery, music, poetry, inspiration and healing, perfection of male beauty, twin brother of Diana. Apollo came to prominence in the 5th century BCE, when the Sibylline Books of Apollo's prophecy (which had been offered to King Tarquinius Superbus by the Sibyl of Cumae) dictated the introduction of His cult in Rome following a plague. Besides Cumae, His oracles were also in other places such as Ionia, Delos, Delphi, Erithrea. It was Apollo who gave the gift of prophecy to His lover Cassandra, who was doomed to speak the truth, but never to be believed. Apollo is father of the God Aesculapius. But Apollo has many aspects, attributes, names and epithets...

Dii Familiaris

The **Lar Familiaris** is the guardian spirit of a family and symbolizes the household. He was honored on all family occasions: a new bride offered a coin and a sacrifice on entering her new house. Rams are sacrificed to the Lar Familiaris after funerals as a purification rite. During the 1st century AD, the Romans came to honor two Lares instead of one, becoming strongly connected with the Penates. In the lararium, the Lares are usually represented in dancing poses, carrying Greek rhytones of wine.

The **Lares Loci** are the guardian spirits of a place. In the lararium, the Lares Loci of the place where the house is built are also honored, being represented by one or more serpents.

Each man has a **Genius**, each woman a **Iuno**. This is the creative force that engenders the individual and imbues him/her with growth, learning and morality. This spirit stays with the person until death. The Genius of the paterfamilias deserves special honor, and is represented in the lararium by a man dressed in white with the head covered by the toga.

The **Penates** are connected with each family. If the family moves, the Penates go with it. They are the spirits of the larder, of food and drink, and they share the hearth as an altar with the Goddess Vesta.

The **Manes** are the spirits of the dead ancestors. When the deceased receives the due honors and rites, he is allowed to ascend from the Underworld to protect his family. This is in contrast with the Lemures or Larvae, evil ghosts which are the souls of the dead who the Dii Inferi refused to receive in the Underworld.

Each corner of the house is under the influence of a protector God. **Forculus** protects the door, **Limentinus** the threshold, **Cardea** the hinges. **Vesta** protects the hearth. Each tool has also its protector spirit: **Deverra** protects the broom, **Pilumnus** the rammer, **Intercidona** the axe.

The generation of a human being is also ruled by protector Gods. **Iuno** and **Mena** assure the menstrual flux of the future mother. **Jugatinus** presides to the union of man and woman. **Cinxia** or **Virginensis** uncover the woman's girdle. **Subigus** delivers her to the man. **Prema** commands the penetration. **Inuus** (**Tutunus** or **Mutunus**) and **Pertunda** put an end to virginity. **Ianus**, God of passage, opens the way for the generating seed emanated from **Saturnus**, but it is Liber who allows the ejaculation. Once **concepted**, the new human being needs **Fluonia** or **Fluvionia**, Who retains the nourishing blood. But the nourishing itself is presided by **Alemona**. To avoid the dangers of upside-down pregnancy, **Postverta** and **Prosa** are invoked. **Diana Nemorensis** is also invoked to allow a good pregnancy. Three deities protect the mother from the violence of **Silvanus**: **Intercidona**, **Deverra** and **Pilumnus**. In the atrium, a bet is setup for **Pilumnus** and **Picumnus** or **Iuno**, and a table is setup for **Hercules**. **Nona** and **Decima** allow the birth between the ninth and tenth month. But it is **Egeria** who makes the baby come out (egerere). **Parca** or **Partula** preside to the birth, but it is **Vitumnus** Who gives life, **Sentinus** the senses. After the birth, **Lucina**, bringer of light, must be invoked. **Lucina** is also the Goddess to whom sterile (or with pregnancy disease) women direct their prayer. After the birth, the pregnant women must be purified, and it is **Iuno Februa** (**Februalis** or **Februlis**) Who frees them from the placental membrane. With the aid of **Levana**, the sage-woman raises and presents the child to the mother. The father then raises the child with the aid of **Statina** (**Statilina**, **Statinus** or **Statilinus**).

Dii Indigetes

There is also a group of mysterious deities formed by native tutelary deities, river gods or deified heroes from Latium which are collectively called **Dii Indigetes** (e.g. deified **Aeneas**, **Faunus**, **Sol Indiges**, **Iuppiter Indiges**, **Numicus**). A multitude of other deities is also traditionally worshipped, which includes tutelary deities (e.g. **Roma**, **Tiberinus**), native Latin deities (e.g. **Bellus**, **Bellona**, **Liber**, **Libera**), abstract deities such as **Fortuna** (Fortune), **Concordia** (Concord), **Pax** (Peace), **Iustitia** (Justice), etc.

Pre-Roman native Italian deities mainly adopted from the Sabines and Etruscans are also worshipped: **Nerio** (Sabine deity and the consort of Mars), **Dius Fidius** (Sabine as well), etc. In fact, **Quirinus** and **Vertumnus** were also adopted respectively from the Sabines and Etruscans.

Other important gods are **Ianus**, **Saturnus**, **Quirinus**, **Volturnus**, **Pales**, **Furrina**, **Flora**, **Carmenta**, **Pomona**, **Portunus** and **Fontanus**.

Dii Novensiles

The pious spirit of the Romans consists of a constant wish to bring the favor of the divine upon him, the family and the state. As such, the Roman is naturally willing to pay the deserved homage and sacrifice to foreign deities, especially if he is in their land. In order to achieve victory in war, the Romans often asked the favor of the gods of their enemies, paying them sacrifices even greater than those offered by their own people.

This spirit joined by the affluence of foreigners which resulted either from trade or conquest, brought new cults to Rome. These were as expected democratically adopted by permitting the priests of these gods to establish temples in Rome. Among the foreign deities, the Dii Novensiles, are **Apollo**, **Ceres** (these were adopted as early as to allow them to become part of the Dii Consentes), **Bacchus** (Dionysus), **Sol Invictus**, **Isis**, **Serapis**, **Magna Mater (Cybele)**, **Attis**, **Mithras** and many others.

Dii Inferi

The Dii Inferi, gods of the Underworld (Inferus) are **Dis (Orcus)** and **Proserpina**, equated to the Greek gods Hades/Pluton (Pluto in Latin) and Persephone. These gods symbolize the creative power of the Earth which provide human beings the means for subsistence (Dis = wealth = Pluton in Greek). The Inferus is also traditionally regarded as the home for the spirits of the dead, though the concept of afterlife was quite varied.

The Roman Pantheon

This is a directory of Roman gods and goddesses, their offspring and consorts, and other minor deities:[1]

Abundantia
A minor Roman goddess of abundance, prosperity and good fortune. Her attribute is a cornucopia ("horn of plenty") with which she distributes grain and money. After the Roman occupation of France, she remained in French folklore as Lady Hobunde.

Acca Larentia
In Roman myth a loose woman and a mistress of Hercules. She married the wealthy Tarutius and after his death she donated his money to the Roman people. In return, Rome celebrated the festival of the Larentalia (possible a feast of the dead in honor of the goddess Larentia) on December 23. In another version, Acca Larentia is the wife of the shepherd Faustulus who raised the twins Romulus and Remus.

Acestes
A hero of Trojan origin, who founded Segesta on Sicily. In a trial of skill Acestes shot his arrow with such force that it took fire. He helped Aeneas when the latter arrived on Sicily after his wanderings.[2]

Achates
A loyal friend and companion of Aeneas.[3]

Acmon
A companion of Aeneas.

Adeona
The Roman goddess who guides the child back home, after it has left the parental house for the first time.

Aequitas
The Roman god of fair dealing.

Aera Cura
The Roman goddess of the infernal regions.

Aeternitas
The Roman personification of eternity. He is symbolized a worm or serpent biting its own tail (similar to the Ouroboros) and by a phoenix rising from its ashes.

Africus
The Roman personification of the south-western wind.

Albunea
A Roman nymph of the sulfuric spring near Tibur (the current Tivoli).

Alemonia
The Roman goddess who feeds the unborn child.

Anchises
Anchises was the son of Capys, and a cousin of King Priam of Troy. He was loved by Venus, who bore him a son, Aeneas. Anchises was the owner of six remarkable horses, which he acquired by secretly mating his own mares with the divinely-bred stallions of Laomedon. But he was chiefly remembered because of the career of his son. After the fall of Troy, Aeneas escaped from the burning ruins of the city, carrying his father and the household gods (see Lares and Penates) on his shoulders. Anchises then accompanied Aeneas and the band of Trojan refugees who set sail for Italy, where it was prophesied that they would found the city of Rome. Anchises died before the trip was over, and was buried in Sicily. After his death, Anchisessaw his son once more, when Aeneas visited the underworld to learn more about his own destiny.

Angerona
The protecting deity of ancient Rome and a goddess of secrecy and of the winter solstice. Angerona is shown with a bandaged mouth with a finger to her lips commanding silence. Her feast -- the Divalia or Angeronalia -- was celebrated on December 21.

Angita
An early Roman goddess of healing and witchcraft.

Angitia
A Roman snake-goddess who was especially worshipped by the Marsi, a tribe in central Italy.

Anna
The daughter of Belus, and sister of Dido. After Dido's death she fled from Africa to Latium, where she was welcomed by Aeneas. Dido's shade warned her for the jealousy of Lavinia, the wife of Aeneas. After hearing this, she threw herself into the river Numicius and drowned. As a river nymph she was later venerated as Anna Perenna. According to some sources, this name has no connection with Dido's sister.

Anna Perenna
The Roman goddess of the new year. Her festival was celebrated on March 15. The Romans gave various explanations to the origin or her name, amnis perennis ("eternal stream"): she was a river nymph; her name was derived from annis ("year"); she was a moon-goddess of the running year; also, she was equated with Anna, the sister of Dido, who was received in Latium by Aeneas, but drowned herself in a river. In the class-struggle between the patricians and plebeians she chose the side of the plebeians.

Annonaria
An alternative name of Fortuna as protector of the corn supplies.

Antevorte
The Roman goddess of the future.

Appiades
The five Roman goddesses who had a temple near the Appian aqueducts. They are Concordia, Minerva, Pax, Venus, and Vesta.

Appias
A Roman nymph. Two fountains dedicated to her flanked the entrance to the temple of Venus Genitrix on the Forum of Caesar in Rome.

Aquilo
The Roman personification of the North Wind. His Greek counterpart is Boreas.

Aurora
Aurora is the Roman personification of the dawn. She is also the Roman equivalent of the Greek goddess Eos. Aurora is seen as a lovely woman who flies across the sky announcing the arrival of the sun. Aurora has two siblings: a brother, the sun, and a sister, the moon. She has had quite a number of husbands and sons. Four of her sons are the four winds (north, south, east, and west). According to one myth, her tears cause the dew as she flies across the sky weeping for one of her sons, who was killed. Aurora is certainly not the most brilliant goddess as she asked Zeus to grant one of her husbands immortality, but forgot to ask for everlasting youth. As a result, her husband soon became aged. Aurora is not one of the better-known goddesses. However, Shakespeare refers to her in his famous play Romeo and Juliet.

Ascanius
Ascanius was the son of Aeneas and Creusa, and the grandson of Venus; he was also called Iulus. He accompanied his father to Italy after the fall of Troy, and fought briefly in the Italian wars. The Julian gens claimed descent from him.

Auster
The personification of the south wind which brought fogs and rain or sultry heat. He is equivalent with the Greek Notus. It is the modern sirocco.

Averna
The Roman queen of the dead

Bacchus
The Roman god of wine and intoxication, equated with the Greek Dionysus. His festival was celebrated on March 16 and 17. The Bacchanalia, orgies in honor of Dionysus, were introduced in Rome around 200 BCE. These infamous celebrations, notorious for their sexual and criminal character, got so out of hand that they were forbidden by the Roman Senate in 186 BCE. Bacchus is also

identified with the old-Italian god Liber.

Bellona
The Roman goddess of war, popular among the Roman soldiers. She accompanied Mars in battle, and was variously given as his wife, sister or daughter. She had a temple on the Capitolinus (inaugurated in 296 BCE and burned down in 48 BCE), where, as an act of war, a spear was cast against the distant enemy. Her festival was celebrated on June 3. Bellona's attribute is a sword and she is depicted wearing a helmet and armed with a spear and a torch. She could be of Etruscan origin, and is identified with the Greek Enyo.

Bona Dea
Bona Dea ("the Good Goddess") is a Roman fertility goddess, especially worshipped by the Roman matrons. She presided over both virginity and fertility in women. She is the daughter of the god Faunus and she herself is often called Fauna. She had a temple on the Aventine Hill, but her secret rites (on December 4) were not held there but in the house of a prominent Roman magistrate. Only women were admitted and even representations of men and beasts were removed. At these secret meetings it was forbidden to speak the words 'wine' and 'myrtle' because Faunus had once made her drunk and beaten her with a myrtle stick. Her festival was observed on May 1. Similarly, no men were allowed to be present here either. She was also a healing goddess and the sick were tended in her temple garden with medicinal herbs. Bona Dea was portrayed sitting on a throne, holding a cornucopia. The snake is her attribute, a symbol of healing, and consecrated snakes were kept in her temple at Rome, indicating her phallic nature. Her image could often be found on coins.

Bubona
The Roman goddess of horses and cattle. She is equal to the Gaulish goddess Epona, whose cult was later adopted by the Roman army.

Caca
The Roman goddess of the hearth and the sister of the fire-breathing giant Cacus. When Heracles returned with the cattle of Geryon, Cacus stole some of the animals and hid them in his cave. According to some sources, out of sympathy for the hero, Caca told

Heracles the location of that cave and he killed the giant. Caca was later succeeded by Vesta.

Cacus

Originally a pre-Roman god of fire, who gradually became a fire-breathing demon. Cacus lived in a cave in the Aventine Hill from where he terrorized the countryside. When Heracles returned with the cattle of Geryon, he passed Cacus' cave and lay down to sleep in the vicinity. At night Cacus dragged some of the cattle to his cave backward by their tails, so that their tracks would point in the opposite direction. However, the lowing of the animals betrayed their presence in the cave to Heracles and he retrieved them and slew Cacus. Other sources claim that Cacus' sister told Heracles the location of his cave. On the place were Heracles slew Cacus he erected an altar, where later the Forum Boarium, the cattle market, was held.

Caeculus

An ancient Italian hero, son of Vulcan. He is regarded as the founder of Praeneste (the current Palestrina).

Camenae

The Camenae were originally ancient Roman goddesses of wells and springs. Later they were identified with the Greek Muses. In Rome, they were worshipped in a sacred forest at the Porta Capena.

Candelifera

The Roman goddess of birth. She is identified with Carmenta and the goddess Lucina.

Canens

A nymph from Latium and the personification of song. She was the wife of king Picus, who was loved by Circe but when he rejected her, Circe transformed him into a woodpecker. After she had wandered for six days without finding him, Canens threw herself from a rock into the Tiber. After one final song she evaporated.

Cardea

The goddess of thresholds and especially door-pivots (cardo "door-pivot"). Just as Carna she is also a goddess of health. Cardea is the protectress of little children against the attacks of vampire-witches. She obtained the office from Janus in exchange for her personal favors. Ovid says of Cardea, apparently quoting a religious formula: 'Her power is to open what is shut; to shut what is open.

Carmenta
Carmenta is the Roman goddess of childbirth and prophecy, one of the Camenae. Her temple (where it was forbidden to wear leather), was in Rome, next to the Porta Carmentalis. Her festival, the Carmentalia, took place on 11 and 15 January, and was mostly celebrated by women. She is the mother of Euander.

Castores
The Roman name of the Dioscuri; from Castor, who seems to have been the first of the twins to be worshipped by the Romans.

Catillus
The brother of the river-deity Tibertus, and co-founder of the city of Tibur (current Tivoli).

Ceres
The old-Italian goddess of agriculture, grain, and the love a mother bears for her child. The cult of Ceres was originally closely connected with that of Tellus, the goddess earth. In later mythology, Ceres is identified with the Greek Demeter. She is the daughter of Saturn and the mother of Proserpina. Ceres had a temple on the Aventine Hill, were she was worshipped together with Liber and Libera. Her festival, the Cerealia, was celebrated on April 19. Ceres is portrayed with a scepter, a basket with flowers or fruits, and a garland made of the ears of corn. Another festival was the Ambarvalia, held in May.

Chnubis
A Roman syncretic god with Greek and Egyptian associations, portrayed as a snake with a lion's head.

Cinxia
The Roman goddess of marriage.

Clementia
The Roman goddess of mercy and clemency.

Clitunno
A Roman river deity.

Cloacina
The goddess who presides of the system of sewers (from the Latin cloaca, "sewer") which drained the refuse of the city of Rome. The main sewer was called Cloaca Maxima.

Coelus
"Sky". The Roman personified god of the heavens who is identified with the Greek Uranus. His wife is Terra.

Concordia
The Roman goddess of concord. She was worshipped in many temples, but the oldest was on the Forum Romanum and dates back to 367 BCE and was built by Camilus. The temple also served as a meeting-place for the Roman senate. Concordia is portrayed sitting, wearing a long cloak and holding a sacrificial bowl in her left hand and a cornucopia in her right. Sometimes she can be seen standing between two members of the Royal House who clasp hands.

Conditor
The Roman god of harvesting the crops.

Consentes Dii
The twelve major gods of the Roman pantheon, identified by the Roman with the Greek Olympians. Six male and six female gods and goddesses. They are: Jupiter and Juno, Neptune and Minerva, Apollo and Diana, Mars and Venus, Vulcan and Vesta, and Mercury and Ceres. Their statues could be found in the hall of the Consentes Dii at the Forum Romanum.

Consus
The Roman god who presides over the storing of grain. Since the grain was stored in holes underneath the earth (near the Circus Maximus). It was uncovered only during the Consualia, his festival

on August 21 and December 15. One of the main events during this festival was a mule race (the mule was his sacred animal). Also on this day, farm and dray horses were not permitted to work and attended the festivities. He is closely connected with the fertility goddess Ops (Ops Consiva). Later he was also regarded as god of secret counsels.

Convector
The Roman god of bringing in the crops.

Copia
The Roman goddess of wealth and plenty, who carried a cornucopia ("horn of plenty"). She belongs to the retinue of Fortuna.

Corus
The Roman god representing the north/north-west wind.

Cuba
The Roman goddess who protects the infants in their cribs and sends them to sleep.

Cumaean Sibyl
The earliest of the Sibyls. She was believed to have come from the rest, and resided at Cumae. She owned, according to tradition, nine books of prophecies. When the Roman king Targuin (Tarquinius Priscus) wanted to buy those books he thought the price she asked far too high. The Sibyl threw three books into the fire and doubled the price; this she did again with the next three books, and the king was forced the buy the remaining three books for a price four times as high as the original nine. makes the victim fall in love. He is also portrayed as a young man with his beloved Psyche, with Venus or with a small group of winged infants (the Amoretti or Amorini). Some traditions say that he was born from a silver egg. His Greek equivalent is Eros. The name is derived from the Latin cupido, "desire".

Cura
A goddess who first fashioned humans from clay.

Curtius

Marcus Curtius, a Roman hero. When one day a gap suddenly appeared on the Forum in Rome, an oracle said that it could only be closed by the most precious thing Rome possessed. The wellbeing of the town depended on it. Curtius sacrificed himself by jumping fully armed and mounted on the finest horse into the gap, which then closed itself. The gap, called the Lacus Curtius is situated at the Forum Romanum. According to other sources, the gap was created when lightning struck, which was then consecrated by the consul Caius Curtius in 445 BCE.[4]

Dea Dia

A Roman goddess of growth, identified with Ceres. Her priests were the Fratres Arvales who honored her in the feast of the Ambarvalia, held in May. During these days, the priests blessed the fields and made offerings to the powers of the underworld.

Dea Tacita

The 'silent goddess'. A Roman goddess of dead.

Decima

A Roman goddess of childbirth. Together with Nona and Morta she forms the Parcae (the Roman goddesses of Fate).

Dei Lucrii

The Roman gods of profit. In time they were superseded by Mercury.

Devera

Devera is the Roman goddess that rules the brooms used to purify ritual sites.

Di Inferi

The Roman deities of the underworld. They were honored with the Ludi Tauri quinquennales, games which took place every five years on June 25 and 26 and which was held at the Circus Flaminius in Rome. The games were, according to legend, instituted to placate the gods of the underworld who were held responsible for sending a plague during the reign of Tarquinius Superbus (534-510 BCE).

Dia
Her name shows that she was one of Italy's original goddesses, but there is little information about her today.

Diana
The Roman goddess of nature, fertility and childbirth. She is closely identified with the Greek goddess Artemis. Diana is also a moon-goddess and was originally worshipped on the mountain Tifata near Capua and in sacred forests (such as Aricia in Latium). Her priest lived in Aricia and if a man was able to kill him with a bough broken from a tree in this forest, he would become priest himself [1]. Also torch-bearing processions were held in her honor here. Later she was given a temple in the working-class area on the Aventine Hill where she was mainly worshipped by the lower class (plebeians) and the slaves, of whom she was the patroness. Slaves could also ask for asylum in her temple. Her festival coincided with the idus (13th) of August. Diana was originally a goddess of fertility and, just as Bona Dea, she was worshipped mainly by women as the giver of fertility and easy births. Under Greek influence she was equated with Artemis and assumed many of her aspects. Her name is possibly derived from 'diviana' ("the shining one"). She is portrayed as a huntress accompanied by a deer. Diana was also the goddess of the Latin commonwealth.

Dii Mauri
The 'Moorish gods' mentioned in Latin inscriptions in North Africa, who are almost never named. They were supposed to be 'salutares' (redemptory), 'immortales' (immortal), and 'augusti' (exalted).

Dirae
Literally "the terrible"; a Latin name for the Furies. The name was mainly used in poetry.

Dis Pater
The Roman ruler of the underworld and fortune, similar to the Greek Hades. Every hundred years, the Ludi Tarentini were celebrated in his honor. The Gauls regarded Dis Pater as their ancestor. The name is a contraction of the Latin Dives, "the wealthy", Dives Pater, "the wealthy father", or "Fater Wealth". It refers to the wealth of precious stone below the earth.

Disciplina
Disciplina is the Roman goddess of discipline.

Discordia
The personified Roman goddess of strife and discord. She belonged to the retinue of Mars and Bellona. She is the Greek Eris.

Dius Fidus
The Roman god of oaths. Dius Fidus is of Sabine origin.

Domiduca
The Roman goddess who escorts the child safely back home.

Domiducus
The Roman god who guides a bride to her new home.

Domitius
The Roman god who kept a woman in the house of her husband.

Duellona
A Roman goddess.

Egeria
The Roman goddess who inspired and guided Numa Pompilius, the successor of Romulus in the kingship of Rome. She is also regarded as his wife. They used to meet in a sacred grove in the midst of which a spring gushed forth and there she taught him wise legislation and the forms of public worship. After his death in 673 BCE she changed into a well in the forest of Aricia in Latium, which was dedicated to Diana. Egeria is one of the Camenae and was also worshipped as a goddess of birth.

Egestes
The Roman personification of poverty. Virgil mentioned her later as a demon in the underworld.

Empanda
This goddess personified the idea of openness and generosity.

Endovelicus
Endovelicus is a native god of the pre-Roman communities (Iron Age) in Lusitania (south west of Iberia) later adopted by the Romans themselves. As a god he was concerned with the good health and welfare of the people. There are hundreds of inscriptions of him in Portugal and Spain.

Erycina
An epithet of Venus because of her worship on mount Eryx on Sicily.

Evander
A minor Roman deity who was believed to have introduced the Greek pantheon, laws, the alphabet, and other arts and skills in Rome.

Eventus Bonus
Eventus Bonus ("good ending") is the Roman god of success in business, but who also ensured a good harvest. His statue stood on the Capitol in Rome, near the temple of Jupiter Optimus Maximus.

Fabulinus
A minor Roman god of infants. Mentioned by Varro, Fabulinus taught Roman children to utter their first word. He received an offering when the child spoke its first words. (From fabulari, to speak.)

Facunditas
The Roman personification of fertility.

Fama
The Roman personified goddess of fame, and the personification of popular rumor. What she heard she repeated first in a whisper to few, then louder and louder until she communicated it to all heaven and earth. Mentioned as a daughter of Tellus. Not truly a goddess, she was more a literary conceit. She had as many eyes, ears, and tongues as she had feathers. Virgil mentions Fama ("rumor") as a horrible creature with multiple tongues and tattling mouths. The Greek version is Pheme.[5]

Fames
The Roman personification of hunger. Virgil mentioned that Fames lived in the underworld, next to Poverty. Ovid wrote that she lived in the inhospitable Scythia.

Fauna
A Roman earth-mother and fertility goddess, usually termed the Bona Dea. She is thought to be the wife, sister or daughter of Faunus. Fauna is identified with Terra, Tellus or Ops.

Fauns
Among the Romans, fauns were wild forest deities with little horns, the hooves of a goat, and a short tail. They accompanied the god Faunus. Fauns are analogous to the Greek satyrs.

Faunus
The god of wild nature and fertility, also regarded as the giver of oracles. He was later identified with the Greek Pan and also assumed some of Pan's characteristics such as the horns and hooves. As the protector of cattle he is also referred to as Lupercus ("he who wards off the wolf"). One particular tradition tells that Faunus was the king of Latium, and the son of Picus. After his death he was deified as Fatuus, and a small cult formed around his person in the sacred forest of Tibur (Tivoli). On February 15 (the founding date of his temple) his feast, the Lupercalia, was celebrated. Priests (called the Luperci) wearing goat skins walked through the streets of Rome and hit the spectators with belts made from goat skin. Another festival was the Faunalia, observed on December 5. He is accompanied by the fauns, analogous to the Greek satyrs. His feminine counterpart is Fauna. The wolf skin, wreath, and a goblet are his attributes.

Faustitas
The goddess who protects the herds.

Faustulus
In Roman myth, the shepherd who found the twins Romulus and Remus on the Palatine Hill where they were reared by a she-wolf. He took them with him and gave them to his wife Acca Larentia to rear.

Favonius
The Roman god of the gentle western wind, the herald of spring. Favonius ("favorable") is equal to the Greek Zephyrus.

Febris
The goddess who protects against fever. Febris ("fever") had three temples in ancient Rome, of which one was located between the Palatine and Velabrum.

Felicitas
The Roman personification of success. Her temples were closely associated with the person of the emperor and one was located on the Forum Romanum.

Ferentina
The goddess of the mountain city of Ferentinum in Latium. She was protector of the Latin commonwealth.

Feronia
The Roman goddess who was invoked to secure a bountiful harvest. She was worshipped in Capena, located at the base of Mount Soracte, and Terracina, and had a temple on the Campus Martius in Rome. She was worshipped as the goddess of freedom by slaves, for it was believed that those who sat on a holy stone in her sanctuary were set free. Her festival took place on November 15.

Fides
The Roman goddess of good faith and faithfulness. She was worshipped as Fides Publica Populi Romani (loyalty towards the Roman state). In her temple on the Capitol the Roman Senate confirmed state treaties with foreign powers, which were kept there under her protection.

Flora
The goddess of blossoming flowers of spring. She had a minor temple on the Quirinalis and was given a sanctuary near the Circus Maximus in 238 BCE. The festival of the Floralia, celebrated on April 28 -May 1, existed until the 4th century CE. Flora is identified with the Greek Chloris.

Fontus
The Roman god of wells and springs, son of Janus and Juturna. The festival of Fontus took place on October 13. He is also called Fons.

Fornax
Fornax ("oven") is the personified Roman goddess of the baking of bread.

Fortuna
The Roman personification of good fortune, originally a goddess of blessing and fertility and in that capacity she was especially worshipped by mothers. Her cult is thought to be introduced by Servius Tullius. She had a temple on the Forum Boarium and a sanctuary, the Fortuna Populi Romani, stood on the Quirinalis. In Praeneste she had an oracle where a small boy randomly choose a little oak rod (sors), upon which a fate was inscribed. Some of Fortuna's names include: Primigenia, Virilis, Respiciens, Muliebris, and Annonaria. She is portrayed standing, wearing a rich dress. The cornucopia, rudder, ball, and blindfold are her attributes. Her Greek counterpart is Tyche.

Fraus
The Roman personification of treachery.

Fulgora
The Roman goddess of lightning.

Furies
The Roman goddess of vengeance. They are equivalent to the Greek Erinyes. The Furies, who are usually characterized as three sisters (Alecto, Tisiphone, and Magaera) are the children of Gaia and Uranus. They resulted from a drop of Uranus' blood falling onto the earth. They were placed in the Underworld by Virgil and it is there that they reside, tormenting evildoers and sinners. However, Greek poets saw them as pursuing sinners on Earth. The Furies are cruel, but are also renowned for being very fair.

Furina
The Roman goddess of thieves.
Furrina

An ancient Roman goddess, who was perhaps a spirit of darkness. Her festival, the Furrinalia, continued to be observed on July 25 in later Roman times, despite the fact that her nature had been forgotten. Her priest was called the flamen Furrinalis. It was in the grove of Furrina that Gaius Sempronius Gracchus ordered his slave to kill him.

Galli
The hierodules or priests of Cybele, who castrated themselves in identification with the goddess. The Roman name for the Corybantes.

Geminus
"Double". An epithet of Janus, referring to his two faces.

Genius / Juno
In Roman mythology, the genius was originally the family ancestor who lived in the underworld. Through the male members he secured the existence of the family. Later, the genius became more a protecting or guardian spirit for persons. These spirits guided and protected that person throughout his life. Every man had a genius, to whom he sacrificed on birthdays. It was believed that the genius would bestow success and intellectual powers on its devotees. Women had their own genius, which was called a juno.

The juno was the protector of women, marriage and birth. It was worshipped under many names: Virginalis (juno of the virgin), Matronalis (of the married woman), Pronuba (of the bride), Iugalis (of marriage), etc. Juno was also the name for the queen of the gods. However, not only individuals had guardian spirits: families, households, and cities had their own. Even the Roman people as a whole had a genius. The genius was usually depicted as a winged, naked youth, while the genius of a place was depicted as a serpent. (See also: Lares.)

Hercules
Hercules, the Latin equivalent of Heracles, was the son of Jupiter and Alcmene. His jealous stepmother, Juno, tried to murder the infant Hercules by putting a serpent in his cradle. Luckily for Hercules, he was born with great strength and killed the serpent. By

the time Hercules was an adult, he had already killed a lion. Eventually, Juno drove Hercules insane. Due to his insanity, Hercules killed his wife, Megara, and their three children. Hercules exiled himself because of the shame that he had brought on himself through his lack of sanity. Hercules decided to ask the Delphic Oracle what he should do to regain his honor. The Oracle told Hercules to go to Eurystheus, king of Mycenae, and serve him for twelve years. King Eurystheus couldn't think of any tasks that might prove difficult for the mighty son of Jupiter, so Juno came down from her palace on Olympus to help him.

Together, the twosome came up with twelve tasks for Juno's mortal stepson to complete. These tasks are now known as the twelve labors of Hercules.

Hercules' first labor was to kill the menacing Nemean Lion; Hercules strangled the creature and carried it back to Mycenae.

The second task was to overcome the nine-headed snake known as the Hydra; Hercules' cousin Ioloas helped him out by burning the stumps of the heads after Hercules cut off the heads; since the ninth head was immortal, Hercules rolled a rock over it.

The third task was to find the golden-horned stag and bring it back alive; Hercules followed the stag around for one full year; he finally captured the stag and took it back alive.

The fourth labor was to capture a wild boar that terrorized Mycenae's people; Hercules chased the boar up a mountain where the boar fell in to a snow drift, where Hercules subdued it.

The fifth task of Hercules was to clean the Augean stables, where thousands of cattle were housed, in a single day; Hercules diverted two rivers so that they would flow into the Augean stables.

The sixth labor was to destroy the man-eating Stymphalian birds; Hercules drove them out of their hiding places with a rattle and shot them with poison-tipped arrows.

The seventh task was for Hercules to capture a Cretean savage bull;

Hercules wrestled it to the ground and took it back to King Eurystheus.

The eighth labor was to capture the four man-eating mares of Thrace; Hercules threw the master of the mares to them; the horses became very tame, so Hercules safely led them back to Mycenae.

Hercules' ninth labor was to obtain the girdle of the fierce Amazon warrior queen, Hippolyta; Hippolyta willingly gave her girdle to Hercules, but Juno convinced the Amazons that Hercules was trying to take Hippolyta from them, so Hercules fought them off and returned to his master with the girdle.

The tenth labor was to capture the cattle of the monster, Geryon; Hercules killed Geryon, claimed the cattle, and took them back to the king.

The eleventh task was to get the golden-apples of the Hesperides; Hercules told Atlas that if he would get the apples for him, he (Hercules) would hold the heavens for him; when Atlas returned from his task, Hercules tricked him into taking back the heavens.

The final labor of Hercules was to bring the three-headed watchdog of the underworld, Cerberus, to the surface without using any weapons; Hercules seized two of Cerberus' heads and the dog gave in. Hercules took the dog to his master, who ordered him to take it back.

Finally, after twelve years and twelve tasks, Hercules was a free man. Hercules went to the town of Thebes and married Deianira. She bore him many children. Later on in their life, the male centaur, Nessus, abducted Deianira, but Hercules came to her rescue by shooting Nessus with a poison tipped arrow. The dying Nessus told Deianira to keep a portion of his blood to use as a love potion on Hercules if she felt that she was losing him to another woman. A couple of a months later, Deianira thought that another woman was coming between her and her husband, so Deianira washed one of Hercules' shirts in Nessus' blood and gave it to him to wear. Nessus had lied to her, for the blood really acted as a poison and almost killed Hercules. On his funeral pyre, the dying

Hercules ascended to Olympus, where he was granted immortality and lived among the gods.

Hersilia
The wife of Romulus. She was, just as her husband, deified after his death.

Herulus
The son of the goddess Feronia. He had three lives and was killed by Evander.

Hippona
The Roman goddess of horses. Her image is derived from the Gallic goddess Epona, whose cult was adopted by the Roman soldiers.

Honos
The Roman deity of morality and military honor. There were several temples devoted to him in Rome. Honos is depicted as a young warrior bearing a lance and a Cornucopia ("horn of plenty").

Horatus Cocles
A legendary hero from the earliest history of Rome. When the Etruscans lay siege to Rome and occupied the Ianiculus Hill, Cocles defended the bridge that led to the city all by himself, against overwhelming odds. Meanwhile the Romans demolished the bridge behind his back and when they were done, he dove into the water and swam to safety.

Imporcitor
The Roman god of the third ploughing. See also Redarator and Vervactor.

Indigites Dii
The group of original, native Roman gods, in contrast to the Novensiles Dii, gods imported from elsewhere. The Indigites Dii were only invoked in special situations. They are the protectors of homes, stables, barns, fields, meadows, et cetera.

Indivia
The Roman goddess of jealousy.

Inferi Dii
The Roman gods of the underworld.

Inuus
The Roman gods of herds.

Italus
An ancient Italian hero, the son of Penelope and Telegonus. He was king of the Oenotrians or of the Siculi, who are regarded as the first inhabitants of Italy.

Iuppiter
See Jupiter below.

Jana
A minor Roman goddess. She is the wife of the god Janus.

Janus
Janus is the Roman god of gates and doors (ianua), beginnings and endings, and hence represented with a double-faced head, each looking in opposite directions. He was worshipped at the beginning of the harvest time, planting, marriage, birth, and other types of beginnings, especially the beginnings of important events in a person's life. Janus also represents the transition between primitive life and civilization, between the countryside and the city, peace and war, and the growing-up of young people. One tradition states that he came from Thessaly and that he was welcomed by Camese in Latium, where they shared a kingdom. They married and had several children, among which the river god Tiberinus (after whom the river Tiber is named). When his wife died, Janus became the sole ruler of Latium. He sheltered Saturn when he was fleeing from Jupiter. Janus, as the first king of Latium, brought the people a time of peace and welfare; the Golden Age. He introduced money, cultivation of the fields, and the laws. After his death he was deified and became the protector of Rome. When Romulus and his associates stole the Sabine Virgins, the Sabines attacked the city. The daughter of one of the guards on the Capitoline Hill betrayed her fellow countrymen and guided the enemy into the city. They attempted to climb the hill but Janus made a hot spring erupt from the ground, and the would-be attackers fled from the city. Ever

since, the gates of his temple were kept open in times of war so the god would be ready to intervene when necessary. In times of peace the gates were closed. His most famous sanctuary was a portal on the Forum Romanum through which the Roman legionaries went to war. He also had a temple on the Forum Olitorium, and in the first century another temple was built on the Forum of Nerva. This one had four portals, called Janus Quadrifons. When Rome became a republic, only one of the royal functions survived, namely that of rex sacrorum or rex sacrificulus. His priests regularly sacrificed to him. The month of January (the eleventh Roman month) is named after him. Janus was represented with two faces, originally one face was bearded while the other was not (probably a symbol of the sun and the moon). Later both faces were bearded. In his right hand he holds a key. The double-faced head appears on many Roman coins, and around the 2nd century BCE even with four faces.

Jove
The genitive form of the name, and specifically in this form, of the sky god Jupiter.

Juno
Protector and special counselor of the Roman state and queen of the gods. She is a daughter of Saturn and sister (but also the wife) of the chief god Jupiter and the mother of Iuventas, Mars, and Vulcan. As the patron goddess of Rome and the Roman empire she was called Regina ("queen") and, together with Jupiter and Minerva, was worshipped as a triad on the Capitol (Juno Capitolina) in Rome. As the Juno Moneta (she who warns) she guarded over the finances of the empire and had a temple on the Arx (one of two Capitoline hills), close to the Royal Mint. She was also worshipped in many other cities, where temples were built in her honor. The primary feast of Juno Lucina, called the Matronalia, was celebrated on March 1. On this day, lambs and other cattle were sacrificed to her. Another festival took place on July 7 and was called Nonae Caprotinae ("The Nones of the Wild Fig"). The month of June was named after her. She can be identified with the Greek goddess Hera and, like Hera, Juno was a majestical figure, wearing a diadem on the head. The peacock is her symbolic animal. A juno is also the protecting and guardian spirit of females.

Jupiter

Jupiter is the supreme god of the Roman pantheon, called dies pater, "shining father". He is a god of light and sky, and protector of the state and its laws. He is a son of Saturn and brother of Neptune and Juno (who is also his wife). The Romans worshipped him especially as Jupiter Optimus Maximus (all-good, all-powerful). This name refers not only to his rulership over the universe, but also to his function as the god of the state who distributes laws, controls the realm and makes his will known through oracles. His English name is Jove. He had a temple on the Capitol, together with Juno and Minerva, but he was the most prominent of this Capitoline triad.

His temple was not only the most important sanctuary in Rome; it was also the center of political life. Here official offerings were made, treaties were signed and wars were declared, and the triumphant generals of the Roman army came here to give their thanks. Other titles of Jupiter include: Caelestis (heavenly), Lucetius (of the light), Totans (thunderer), Fulgurator (of the lightning). As Jupiter Victor he led the Roman army to victory. Jupiter is also the protector of the ancient league of Latin cities. His attribute is the lightning bolt and the eagle is both his symbol and his messenger. Jupiter is completely identical with the Greek Zeus.

Justitia

The Roman goddess of justice, portrayed as a woman holding a cornucopia and scales. Later she is portrayed with a blindfold, holding scales and a sword (or scepter).

Juturna

The Roman goddess of wells and springs, sister of Turnus (the king of Rutuli) whom she supported in his battle against Aeneas. Jupiter turned her into a nymph and gave her a well near Lavinium in Latium. She also gave her name to a well near the Vesta-temple of the Forum Romanum, called the Lacus Iuturnae. The water from this well was used for the state-offerings. Also, the Dioscuri were thought to have watered their horses here. She is the mother of Fontus (Fons) and wife of Janus.

Iuventas
"Youth". An early Roman goddess of youth, equal to the Greek goddess Hebe. Boys offered a coin to her when they wore a man's toga for the first time. The temple of Iuventas on the Capitol was more ancient than that of Jupiter. She also had a second temple in the Circus Maximus.

Lactans
The Roman god of agriculture of whom it was said that he made the crops 'yield milk' (thrive).

Lara
Lara is a nymph who betrayed the love affair of Jupiter and Juturna. As punishment, the chief god struck her with dumbness. She is regarded as the mother of the Lares.

Larenta
The Roman earth-goddess, also called Dea Tacita, the silent goddess. Her festival, called the Larentalia, was observed on December 23. On this day offerings were brought to her in a mundus, a opened groove.

Lares
Roman guardian spirits of house and fields. The cult of the Lares is probably derived from the worshipping of the deceased master of the family. It was believed that he blessed the house and brought fertility to the fields. Just like the Penates, the Lares were worshipped in small sanctuaries or shrines, called Lararium, which could be found in every Roman house. They were placed in the atrium (the main room) or in the peristylium (a small open court) of the house. Here people sacrificed food to the Lares on holidays. In contrast to their malignant counterparts the Larvae (Lemures), the Lares are beneficent and friendly spirits. There were many different types of guardians. The most important are the Lares Familiares (guardians of the family), Lares Domestici (guardians of the house), Lares Patrii and Lares Privati. Other guardians were the Lares Permarini (guardians of the sea), Lares Rurales (guardians of the land), Lares Compitales (guardians of crossroads), Lares Viales (guardians of travelers) and Lares Praestitis (guardians of the state). The Lares are usually depicted as dancing youths, with a horn cup

in one hand and a bowl in the other. As progenitors of the family, they were accompanied by symbolic phallic serpents.

Larvae
The Larvae are Roman spirits of deceased family members. These malignant spirits dwell throughout the house and frighten the inhabitants. People tried to reconcile or avert the Larvae with strange ceremonies which took place on May 9, 11, and 13; this was called the "Feast of the Lemures". The master of the house usually performed these ceremonies, either by offering black beans to the spirits or chasing them away by making a lot of noise. Their counterparts are the Lares, friendly and beneficent house spirits.

Latarius
"God of Latium", an epithet of Jupiter.

Latinus
The son of Faunus and the nymph Marica. He was the king of Laurentum in Latium and ancestor of the Latini. According to Roman myth he had welcomed Aeneas, who returned from exile, and offered the hero the hand of his daughter Lavinia.[6]

Latona
The Roman name of Leto. Leto, the daughter of the Titans Phoebe and Coeus. Known as the hidden one and bright one, her name came to be used for the moon Selene. Hera was jealous of Leto because Zeus, the husband of Hera, had fallen in love with her. From their union Leto bore the divine twins, Artemis and Apollo. Leto found this to be an arduous task, as Hera had refused Leto to give birth on either terra firma or on an island out at sea. The only place safe enough to give birth was Delos because Delos was a floating island. Therefore, Leto did not refute the wishes of Hera.

In some versions, Leto was refused by other vicinities because they feared the great power of the god she would bear. To show her gratitude, Leto anchored Delos to the bottom of the Aegean with four columns, to aid its stability. A conflict of legends arises when in one version it says that Artemis was born one day before Apollo, and the birth took place on the island of Ortygia. Then the next day, Artemis helped Leto to cross to the island of Delos, and aided

Leto with the delivery of Apollo. Leto, being the mother of Artemis and Apollo, figured as the motive for the slaughter was Niobe's children was that Niobe had been bragging to Leto about bearing fourteen children (in some versions six or seven). Leto had only born two, and to make matters worse, Niobe then had the audacity to say, it must make her more significant than Leto. When the divine twins were told of this insult, they killed all Niobe's children with their deadly arrows. After which Niobe wept for her dead children so much that she turned into a pillar of stone. From one version of how Apollo slew the monster Python, it was said that while Leto was still pregnant with the divine twins, Python tried to molest her. As punishment, Apollo killed him and then took control of the oracle of Delphi. Leto was worshiped throughout Greece, but principally in Lycia (Asia Minor). In Delos and Athens, there were temples dedicated to her, although in most regions she was worshiped in conjunction with her children, Artemis and Apollo. In Egypt there is the Temple of Leto (Wadjet) at Buto, which was described by Herodotus as being connected to an island which floated. On this island (Khemmis) stood a temple to Apollo, but Herodotus dismissed the claim that it floated as merely the legend of Delos brought to Egypt from Greek tradition. The Romans called Leto "Latona".

Laverna
The Roman goddess of unlawfully obtained profits and therefore a goddess of thieves, imposters and frauds. Her sanctuary in Rome was near the Porta Lavernalis.

Lavinia
The daughter of Latinus and Amata. Although she was engaged to Turnus, king of the Rutuli, she was given by her father to Aeneas as his bride. This resulted in a grim battle between Turnus and Aeneas, which is described by Virgil in one of his last books of the epic 'Aeneas', and which ended with the death of Turnus. Aeneas married Lavinia and she gave birth to Silvius. The city Aeneas founded in Latium, called Lavinium, was named after her.

Letum
A monster which lives in the underworld. The name means 'death'.

Levana
Levana ("lifter") is the protector of newborn babes. The father recognized his child by lifting it from the ground, where it was placed by the mother.

Liber
The old-Italian god of fertility and growth in nature. In later times Liber ("the free one") was equated with Dionysus and became thus a god of viniculture. His feminine counterpart is Libera. Their festival, the Liberia, was observed on March 17.

Liber Pater
The Roman god of fertility, both human and agricultural. He is closely connected with Dionysus.

Libera
A Roman goddess, wife of Liber. She is later equated with Proserpina.
Liberalitas
The Roman god of generosity.

Libertas
The Roman goddess of freedom. Originally as goddess of personal freedom, she later became the goddess of the Roman commonwealth. She had temples on the Aventine Hill and the Forum. Libertas was depicted on many Roman coins as a female figure with a pileus (a felt cap, worn by slaves when they were set free), a wreath of laurels and a spear.

Libitina
The Roman goddess of corpses and the funeral, her name often being a synonym for death itself. In her temple all the necessary equipment for burials were kept. Here, people could rent these attributes as well as grave diggers. Later she was equated with Proserpina.

Lima
The Roman goddess of thresholds.

Lua
The goddess to whom the Romans offered captured weapons by ritually burning them.

Lucina
The Roman goddess of childbirth, who eased the pain and made sure all went well. Lucina became later an epithet of Juno, as "she who brings children into the light" (Latin: lux).

Luna
The personified goddess of the moon. Later she is identified with Diana and Hecate. Her temple, on the Aventine Hill, was erected in the 6th century BCE but was destroyed by the great fire under Nero's regime. She is equivalent to the Greek Selene.

Lupercus
The Roman god of agriculture and shepherds, also an epithet of Faunus. The Luperci sacrificed two goats and a dog on the festival of the Lupercalia, celebrated on February 15. This took place in the Lupercal, a cave were, according to tradition, the twins Romulus and Remus were reared by a wolf. This cave is located at the base of the Palatine Hill. Goats were used since Lupercus was a god of shepherds, and the dog as protector of the flock.

Magna Mater
The Roman name for the Phrygian goddess Cybele, but also an appellation of Rhea. The full name was Magna Mater deorum Idaea: Great Mother of the gods, who was worshipped on Mount Ida. The cult spread through Greece from the 6th to 4th century, and was introduced in Rome in 205 BCE.

Maia
The goddess of whom the month of May is probably named after. Offerings were made to her in this month. She is associated with Vulcan and sometimes equated with Fauna and Ops.

Maiesta
The Roman goddess of honor and reverence, and the wife of the god Vulcan. Some sources say that the month of May is named after her. Others say she is the goddess Maia.

Manes
Manes or Di Manes ("good ones") is the euphemistic description of the souls of the deceased, worshipped as divinities. The formula D.M. (= Dis Manibus; "dedicated to the Manes-gods") can often be found on tombstones. Manes also means metaphorically 'underworld' or 'realm of death'. Festivals in honor of the dead were the Parentalia and the Feralia, celebrated in February.

Mania
Mania was known as the Roman goddess of the dead. She is also the guardian of the underworld, together with Mantus. Mania -- the name -- is the Greek personification of madness. In addition, she is called the mother or grandmother of ghosts. She is also considered the mother of the Lares and Nanes, the gods of the household.

Marica
An Italian nymph, the consort of Faunus and mother of Latinus[7] According to others, she was the mother of Faunus. She possessed a sacred forest near Minturnae (Minturno) on the border of Latium and Campania[8]. A lake near Minturnae was named after her.

Mars
The god of war, and one of the most prominent and worshipped gods. In early Roman history he was a god of spring, growth in nature, and fertility, and the protector of cattle. Mars is also mentioned as a chthonic god (earth-god) and this could explain why he became a god of death and finally a god of war. He is the son of Jupiter and Juno. According to some sources, Mars is the father of Romulus and Remus by the Vestal Ilia (Rhea Silvia). Because he was the father of these legendary founders of Rome, and thus of the Roman people, the Romans styled themselves 'sons of Mars'. His main sanctuaries where the temple on the Capitol, which he shared with Jupiter and Quirinus, the temple of Mars Gradivus ("he who precedes the army in battle") where the Roman army gathered before they went to war, and the temple of Mars Ultor ("the avenger"), located on the Forum Augustus. The Campus Martius ("field of Mars"), situated beyond the city walls, was also dedicated to him. Here the army was drilled and athletes were trained. In the Regia on the Forum Romanum, the 'hastae Martiae' ("lances of Mars") were kept. When these lances 'moved', it was

seen as a portent of war. The warlord who was to lead the army into battle had to move the lances while saying 'Mars vigila' ("Mars awaken"). As Mars Gradivus, the god preceded the army and led them to victory. He had several festivals in his honor. On March 1, the Feriae Marti was celebrated. The Armilustrium was held on October 19, and on this day the weapons of the soldiers were ritually purified and stored for winter. Every five years the Suovetaurilia was held. During these fertility and cleansing rites, a pig (sus), a sheep (ovis) and bull (taurus) were sacrificed. The Equirria were on February 27 and March 14, on which horse races were held. The Quinquatrus was on March 19 and the Tubilustrium on March 23, on which weapons and war-trumpets were cleansed. The priests of Mars, who also served Quirinus, were called the Salii ("jumpers"), derived from the procession through the streets of the city which they completed by jumping the entire way and singing the Carmen Saliare. Mars' own priest was called the flamen Martialis.

Mars is portrayed as a warrior in full battle armor, wearing a crested helmet and bearing a shield. His sacred animals are the wolf and the woodpecker, and he is accompanied by Fuga and Timor, the personifications of flight and fear. The month March (Martius) is named after him (wars were often started or renewed in spring). His Greek equivalent is the god Ares.

Matronae
The three mother-goddess of Roman mythology who oversee fertility. They are lovers of peace, tranquility and children.

Matuta
The Roman goddess of the dawn. Later she was known as Mater Matuta, the patroness of newborn babes, but also of the sea and harbors. Her temple was situated on the Forum Boarium (the cattle market). Every June 11, the Matralia was celebrated here. This festival was only open to women who were still in their first marriage. She was associated with Aurora and identified with the Greek Eos.

Mavors
An ancient and poetic name for Mars.[9]

Meditrina
A Roman goddess of wine and health whose name means "healer". Her festival, the Meditrinalia, was observed on October 11.

Mefitis
The Roman goddess who was especially worshipped in volcanic areas and swamps. She is the personification of the poisonous vapors of the earth.

Melite
A Roman sea nymph.[10]

Mellona
The Roman divinity who protects the bees. Her name is derived from mel ("honey").

Mena
The Roman goddess of menstruation.

Mens
The Roman goddess of mind and consciousness. Her festival was observed on May 8.

Mephitis
A Roman goddess who was particularly worshipped regions with volcanoes or solfataras (volcanic vents emitting hot gases and vapors). She was called upon to protect against damages and poisonous gases).

Mercury
Mercury is god of trade and profit, merchants and travelers, but originally of the trade in corn. In later times he was equated with the Greek Hermes. He had a temple in Rome near the Circus Maximus on the Aventine Hill which dates back to 495 BCE. This temple was connected to some kind of trade fair. His main festival, the Mercuralia, was celebrated on May 15 and on this day the merchants sprinkled their heads and their merchandise with water from his well near the Porta Capena. During the time of the Roman Empire the cult of Mercury was widely spread, especially among the Celtic and Germanic peoples. The Celts have their Gaulish Mercury,

and the Germans identified him with their Wodan. The attributes of Mercury are the caduceus (a staff with two intertwined snakes) and a purse (a symbol of his connection with commerce). He is portrayed similarly to Hermes: dressed in a wide cloak, wearing talaria (winged sandals) and petasus (winged hat). Mercury is also known as Alipes ("with the winged feet").

Messor
Messor ("mower") is the Roman god agriculture, and especially of mowing.

Minerva
The Roman goddess of wisdom, medicine, the arts, dyeing, science and trade, but also of war. As Minerva Medica she is the patroness of physicians. She is the daughter of Jupiter. In the temple on the Capitoline Hill she was worshipped together with Jupiter and Juno, with whom she formed a powerful triad of gods. Another temple of her was located on the Aventine Hill. The church of Santa Maria sopra Minerva is built on one of her temples.

Every year from March 19 - 23 the Quinquatria was held, the primary Minerva-festival. This festival was mainly celebrated by artisans but also by students. On June 13 the minor Quinquatrus was observed. Minerva is believed to be the inventor of numbers and musical instruments. She is thought to be of Etruscan origin, as the goddess Menrva or Menerva. Later she was equated with the Greek Athena.

Moneta
A Roman goddess of prosperity.

Mors
The personified Roman god of death. It is a translation of Thanatos.

Morta
The Roman goddess of death. She is one of the Parcae.

Mulciber
"The softener". A surname of the smith-god Vulcan and alluding to the softening of metals in his fiery forge.

Murcia
A Roman goddess of indistinct origin and of whom is little known. As Murtia she was sometimes equated with Venus. She had a temple in the vale between the Aventine and the Palatine Hill.

Muta
The Roman personification of silence, and its goddess.

Mutinus Mutunus
A Roman fertility god who was invoked by women seeking to bear children. He was depicted as ithyphallic or as a phallus. Also the Roman form (Mutinus) of the Greek Priapus.

Naenia
Naenia is the Roman goddess of funerals.

Nascio
One of the many Roman goddesses of birth.

Necessitas
Necessitas ("necessity") is a Roman goddess of destiny. She is similar to the Greek Ananke.

Nemestrinus
A Roman god of the woods.

Neptune
The god of the sea among the Romans. He was not a very powerful god, and little is known of his origin. When he was first introduced in Rome, he already had all the characteristics of the Greek Poseidon. Despite the fact that his cult grew after his equation with Poseidon, Neptune was far less popular among sailors than Poseidon was among the Greek mariners.

Neptune was held in much higher regard as Neptune Equester, the god and patron of horse-racing and horses. One of temples was located near the Circus Flaminius, one of the larger trace-tracks. Another sanctuary was in the Campus Martius (25 BCE) were the Neptunalia was celebrated on July 23. The trident is Neptune's attribute.

Nerio
A minor Roman goddess, and the consort of Mars.

Nixi
Roman divinities who were invoked by women in labor and who assisted in giving birth (from the Latin nitor, "give birth to").

Nodutus
The Roman god who was held responsible for making the knots in the stalks of corn.

Nona
The Roman goddess of pregnancy. Nona ("ninth") was called upon by a pregnant mother in the ninth month when the child was due to be born. In later times she became associated with the goddesses Morta and Decima and formed the Parcae, the Roman Fates.

Novensilus
The Roman appellation of the nine great gods of the Etruscans.

Nox
"Night". The Roman personification of the night[11]

Nundina
The Roman goddess of the ninth day, on which the newborn child received its name.

Obarator
The Roman god of ploughing.

Occator
The Roman god of harrowing.

Ops
The Roman (Sabine) goddess of the earth as a source of fertility, and a goddess of abundance and wealth in general (her name means "plenty"). As goddess of harvest she is closely associated with the god Consus. She is the sister and wife of Saturn. One of her temples was located near Saturn's temple, and on August 10 a festival took place there. Another festival was the Opalia, which was

observed on December 9.

On the Forum Romanum she shared a sanctuary with the goddess Ceres as the protectors of the harvest. The major temple was of Ops Capitolina, on the Capitoline Hill, where Caesar had located the Treasury. Another sanctuary was located in the Regia on the Forum Romanun, where also the Opiconsivia was observed on August 25. Only the official priests and the Vestal Virgins had access to this altar.

Orbona
The Roman goddess invoked by parents who became childless, and begged her to grant them children again.

Orcus
The Roman god of death and the underworld, either a terrible god or a gentle one. He is the god of oaths and punisher of perjurers. Orcus is identical to the Greek Hades, both the god and his domains.

Pales
The Roman patron goddess of shepherds and flocks. Pales also presides over the health and fertility of the domestic animals. Her festival is the Palilia (also called the Parilia) and was celebrated by shepherds on April 21, the legendary founding date of Rome. On that day large fires were made through which they drove the cattle. Pales was originally a single deity, variously male or female, with the same characteristics. The name is believed by some to be related to the Greek and Latin word phallus.

Palici
The twin sons of Jupiter and the nymph Thalia. They were chthonic deities worshipped at the Palica, near Mount Etna. In early times humans were sacrificed to them and oaths were verified through divine judgment.

Parcae
The Parcae are the Roman goddess of fate, similar to the Greek Moirae (Fates). Originally there was only one of them, Parca, a goddess of birth. Her name is derived from parere ("create, give

birth") but later it was associated with pars (Greek: moira, "part") and thus analogous with the three Greek Moirae. The three Parcae are also called Tria Fata.

Partula
A minor Roman goddess of birth. She is concerned with the parturition.

Patalena
The Roman deity who protects the blossoms.

Paventia
The Roman goddess who protects children against sudden fright.

Pax
Pax ("peace") is the personified Roman goddess of peace, corresponding with the Greek Eirene. Under the rule of Augustus, she was recognized as a goddess proper. She had a minor sanctuary, the Ara Pacis, on the Campus Martius, and a temple on the Forum Pacis. A festival in her honor was celebrated on January 3. Her attributes are the olive branch, a cornucopia, and a scepter.

Penates
In Roman mythology, the Penates ("the inner ones") are the patron gods of the storeroom. Later they gradually changed into patron gods for the entire household. Their cult is closely related to that of Vesta and the Lares. They were worshipped at the hearth and were given their part of the daily meals. The Roman state had its own Penates, called Penates Publici. They were rescued by Aeneas from burning Troy and via Lavinium and Longa brought to Rome. Upon their arrival, the Penates were housed in the Temple of Vesta, on the Forum Romanum.

Picumnus
Picumnus is a minor Roman god of growth and the fertility of the fields. He is the patron of matrimony and infants at birth and stimulated their growth. He is also worshipped as Sterquilinus (or Stercutus) because he invented the manuring of the fields.

Picus
The ancient Roman deity of agriculture. He also possessed the powers of prophecy. He was changed into a woodpecker by Circe when he did not requite her passion.

Pietas
The Roman personification of feelings of duty towards the gods, the state and one's family. Her temple at the foot of the Capitoline Hill dates from the beginning of the second century BCE.

Pilumnus
Pilumnus is a minor Roman god, the brother of Picumnus and together they stimulated the growth of little children and avert sickness. To ensure to help of these gods, people made an extra bed right after the birth of a child. Pilumnus is also believed to have taught mankind how to grind corn.

Pluto
Pluto is the Roman god of the underworld and the judge of the dead. Pluto was the son of Saturn. Pluto's wife was Proserpina (Greek name, Persephone) whom he had kidnapped and dragged into the underworld. His brothers were Jupiter and Neptune. People referred to Pluto as the rich one because he owned all the wealth in the ground. People were afraid to say his real name because they were afraid it might attract his attention. Black sheep were offered to him as sacrifices. Pluto was known as a pitiless god because if a mortal entered his Underworld they could never hope to return. Pluto's Greek name is Hades.

Pluvius
Literally, "sender of rain", an epithet of the Roman god Jupiter. During long droughts the ancient Romans called upon Jupiter using that name. It is also an epithet of the Hyades.

Poena
The Roman goddess of punishment.

Pomona
The goddess presiding over fruit trees. She was the beloved of many ancient Roman rustic deities such as Silvanus and Picus until

Vertumnus, disguised as an old woman, goaded her into marrying him. Her special priest is the flamen Pomonalis. The pruning knife is her attribute.

Portunes

The Roman god of ports and harbors, identified with the Greek Palaemon or Melicertes. Originally he was a god of keys and doors and domestic animals. He protects the warehouses where grain is stored, and is as such a god of the harbors. His temple was located near the Forum Boarium. The Portunalia were observed on August 17, and on this festival keys were thrown into the fire to safeguard them against misfortune. His attribute is a key.

Porus

The Roman god of plenty.

Postverta

The Roman goddess of the past.

Potina

The Roman goddess associated with the first drink of children or children's potions.

Priapus

The Roman patron god of gardens, viniculture, sailors and fishermen. He is portrayed wearing a long dress that leaves the genitals uncovered. The Romans placed a satyr-like statue of him, painted red and with an enormous phallus, in gardens as some kind of scarecrow, but also to ensure fruitfulness. The fruits of the fields, honey and milk were offered to him, and occasionally donkeys. He was very popular and in his honor the Priapea was written--a collection of 85 perfectly written poems, sometimes funny but usually obscene. Originally, Priapus was a fertility god from Asia Minor, especially in Lampsacus on the Hellespont, and was the most important god of the local pantheon (see: the Greek Priapus). He was introduced in Greece around 400 BCE but never was very popular. Priapus' attribute is the pruning knife.

Promitor

The Roman god associated with the bringing out of the harvest from the barns.

Prorsa Postverta
The Roman double-goddess who was called upon by women in labor. She guarded over the position of the child in the womb (forwards or backwards). Some sources mention her as another aspect of Carmenta.

Proserpina
The Roman name for the Greek Persephone. The name is possibly derived from proserpere ("to emerge"), meaning the growing of the grain. Gradually, Libera was equated with her.

Providentia
The Roman goddess of forethought.

Pudicitia
Literally, "modesty". The personified Roman goddess of modesty and chastity.

Puta
A Roman goddesses who watched over the pruning of vines and trees.

Quirinus
An old Roman deity whose origin is uncertain, and there is also little known about his cult. He was worshipped by the Sabines, an old Italian people who lived north-east of Rome. They had a fortified settlement near Rome, the Quirinal, which was named after their god. Later, when Rome expanded, this settlement was absorbed by the city, and Quirinus became, together with Jupiter and Mars, the god of the state. The Quirinalis, one of the Roman hills, was named after him. His consort is Hora. He was usually depicted as a bearded man who wears clothing that is part clerical and part military. His sacred plant is the myrtle. His festival, the Quirinalia, was celebrated on February 17. Romulus was also identified with Quirinus, especially in the late-Roman era[12].

Quiritis
Quiritis is a Sabine protective goddess of motherhood.

Rederator
The Roman god of the second ploughing. See also Imporcitor and Vervactor.

Rederator
The Roman god of the second ploughing. See also Imporcitor and Vervactor.

Remus
The twin brother of Romulus. He was killed by his brother during a quarrel.[13]

Rhea Silvia
The Vestal virgin who became, by Mars, the mother of the twins Romulus and Remus. She is the daughter of king Numitor of Alba Longa, who was dethroned by his brother Amulius. Her uncle gave her to the goddess Vesta so she would remain a virgin for the rest of her life. Amulius had learned from an oracle that her children would become a threat to his power. However, because she had violated her sacred vow, she and her children were cast in the Tiber. The god Tiberinus rescued her and made her his wife.[14]

Robigo
A Roman goddess of corn. She is probably the feminine form of Robigus.

Robigus
The Roman god who protected the corn against diseases. Robigus ("wheat rust", "mildew") was worshipped together with Flora. His festival, the Robigalia, took place on April 25. His functions were also attributed to the female goddess Robigo.

Roma
The personification of the city of Rome. She is portrayed as a helmed woman sitting on a throne, holding a spear and a sword. Resting against her throne is a shield. Her head was commonly depicted on coins, symbolizing the Roman state. Her temple and the temple of Venus were situated on the Velian Hill in Rome. Hadrianus started building it in 121 CE and the temple was inaugurated around 140 CE by Antonius Pius.

Romulus

Romulus and Remus were the twin sons of Rhea Silvia and Mars. They were, together with their mother, cast into the Tiber. The god Tiberinus saved Rhea Silvia from drowning, and the brothers were miraculously rescued by a she-wolf. The wolf reared the twins together with her cubs underneath a fig tree (the 'ruminalus ficus'). After a few years they were found by the shepherd Faustulus, who took the brothers home and gave them to his wife Acca Larentia to raise. When they reached maturity they killed Amelius, the brother of their grandfather, and built a settlement on the Palatine Hill. During a quarrel where Remus mocked the height of the walls, Romulus slew Remus and became the sole ruler of the new Rome, which he had named after himself. He took Hersilia as his wife. To enlarge his empire, he allowed exiles and refugees, homicides and runaway slaves to populate the area. The shortage of women he solved by stealing Sabine women whom he invited to a festival. After a few wars, the Sabines agreed to accept Romulus as their king. Upon his death he was taken to the heavens by his father Mars. He is later revered as the god Quirinus.

Rumina

The Roman protector of nursing mothers and suckling infants, both human and animal. She had a temple near the Ficus Ruminales, the fig tree on the Palatine Hill were Romulus and Remus were reared by a she-wolf. When the tree started to droop in 58 CE this was seen as a bad portent.

Runcina

A Roman deity associated with reaping.

Rusina

A Roman divinity who protects the fields (also known as Rusor).

Sabus

The son of Sancus, the oldest king of the Sabines, who worshipped him as a god.

Salacia

A Roman sea goddess. The god Neptune wanted to marry her but she ran off and hid from him in the Atlantic ocean. Neptune sent a dolphin to look for her and when the animal found her it brought her back to him. Salacia agreed to marry Neptune and the dolphin was awarded a place in the heavens. Salacia bore Neptune three children. She is identified with the Greek god, Amphitrite.

Salus

Salus ("salvation") is the personified Roman goddess of health and prosperity, both of the individual and the state. As Salus Publica Populi Romani ("goddess of the public welfare of the Roman people") she had a temple on the Quirinal, inaugurated in 302 BCE[15]. Later she became more a protector of personal health. Around 180 BCE sacrificial rites in honor of Apollo, Aesculapius, and Salus took place there[16]. Her attribute was a snake or a bowl and her festival was celebrated on March 30. Salus is identified with the Greek Hygieia.

Sancus

An ancient Roman deity who presides over oaths and good faith. He is also called Semo Sancus Dius Fidus.

Saritor

The Roman god of weeding and hoeing.

Saturn

The Roman god of agriculture concerned with the sowing of the seeds. He is regarded as the father of Jupiter, Ceres, Juno and many others. His wife is the goddess Ops. Jupiter supposedly chased him away and he was taken in by the god Janus in Latium where he introduced agriculture and viniculture. This event heralded a period of peace, happiness and prosperity, the Golden Age. In memory of this Golden Age, each year the Saturnalia was observed on December 17 at his temple on the Forum Romanum. This temple, below the Capitoline Hill, contained the Royal Treasury and is one of the oldest in Rome.

The Saturnalia was one of the major events of the year. Originally only one day, it was later extended to seven days. During this festival, business was suspended, the roles of master and slaves were reversed, moral restrictions were loosened and gifts were exchanged. Offerings made in his honor were done with uncovered heads, contrary to the Roman tradition. In contrast to his festival, Saturn himself was never very popular. From the 3rd century on, he was identified with the Greek Cronus, and his cult became only marginally more popular. That he ruled over the Golden Age is an extension to the Greek myth. Saturday is named after him.

Semonia
The Roman goddess of sowing.

Sentia
The Roman goddess who brought about a young child's first awareness.

Sergestus
One of the companions of Aeneas. He was the ancestor of the gens Sergia, a renowned Patrician family of Rome, to whom also Catilina belonged[17].

Silvanus
The Roman god of forests, groves and wild fields. As fertility god he is the protector of herds and cattle and is associated with Faunus. He shows many similarities with the Greek Pan (Silvanus also liked to scare lonely travelers). The first fruits of the fields were offered to him, as well as meat and wine--a ritual women were not allowed to witness. His attributes are a pruning knife and a bough from a pine tree.

Silvius
The son of Aeneas and Lavinia. He was the successor of Ascanius as the king of Alba Longa.[18].

Sol
The personified Roman god of the sun, completely identical to the Greek Helios. He was possibly worshipped as Sol Indiges in his temple on the Quirinalis. A second temple was located at the Circus Maximus, near the race-tracks, where he was considered to be the protector of the four-in-hands which joined the races. The emperor Heliogabalus imported the cult of Sol Invictus ("the invincible sun") from Syria and Sol was made god of the state.

Somnus
The Roman god of sleep, a translation of the Greek Hypnos. Somnus caused the death of Palunurus, the helmsman of Aeneas, who fell asleep at the coast of Lucania[19]
.
Soranus
A Sabine sun-god who was venerated at Mount Soracte (north of Rome). His priests were called the Hirpi Sorani ("wolfs of Soranus") who celebrated a rite in which they walked barefoot on burning coals. Virgil identified Soranus with Apollo (as Apollo Soranus)[20]. At the foot of the Soracte was the precinct of Feronia.

Sors
A Roman god of luck.

Spes
The personified Roman goddess of hope. She had a sanctuary on the vegetable market. Spes is portrayed as a young woman holding a cornucopia and a flower.

Spiniensis
The Roman god who was called upon when people removed thorns from the fields. The name is derived from spina ("spine").

Stata Mater
The Roman goddess who guards against fires, and was thus associated with Vulcan. She was at times equated with Vesta. A statue of Stata Mater was located on the Forum.

Statanus
The Roman god who, together with his wife Statina, watched over the first time a child went away and returned.

Stator
An alternative name of Jupiter as the god who halted retreat or flight (stare - standing). In Rome there were two temples of Jupiter Stator. The oldest (on the Velia Hill) was, according to legend, built by Romulus himself during the war against the Sabeans, when the Romans where forced to retreat[21]. The simple sanctuary of Romulus was replaced by a proper temple in 294 BCE [22] .

Stercutus
A Roman god who took care of the fertilization of farmland (stercus, manure). An alternative name of Saturn or, according to others, Picumnus.

Stimula
The Roman goddess who incites passion in women (especially in the Bacchae). She is equated with the Greek Semele.

Strenua
The Roman goddess of strength and vigor, of Sabine origin. She was worshipped in Rome at the beginning of the new year. Her sanctuary was in the Via Sacra.

Suadela
The goddess of persuasion, and especially in love. She is a follower of Venus.

Subruncinator
The Roman god of weeding.

Summanus
The Roman god of nightly thunder (Jupiter is the god of thunder during daytime). Sammunas' temple stood at the Circus Maximus and on June 20 cakes were offered to him. Probably of Etruscan or Sabean origin. A Roman or Etruscan marital demon who was called upon when the bride was taken to the house of the groom. He is supposed to have been a friend of Romulus and played a part in the stealing of Sabine women. The term 'Talassio' was used when the bride entered her new house[23]

Terra
"Earth". The personified Roman goddess of the earth. She is also a fertility goddess, known as Bona Dea.

Terra Mater
The Roman 'mother earth', the goddess of fertility and growth. Her most prominent festival was the Fordicidia on April 15 where cows being with young were sacrificed. Another festival was the Feriae Sementivae ("the sowing feast in January") where offering where

made to her and Ceres before harvesting.

Tiberinus
The Roman god of the river Tiber. When Aeneas and his Trojan exiles arrived in Latium, the god assisted them. Later Tiberinus also appeared to Aeneas to give him advise. The Volturnia was his festival. His is the father of Ocnus with Manto. There existed a cult of Tiberinus in the early days of Rome, but practically nothing is known about it now.

Tibertus
The god of the river Anio, a tributary of the Tiber. Legend has it that he founded the Italian city Tibur (Tivoli).

Trivia
In Roman mythology, Trivia is the personified deity of crossroads, derived from the Latin trivium ("meeting of three roads"). She was represented with three faces, and sometimes identified with the Greek Hecate.

Ultor
A title given to Mars when, after defeating the murderers of Julius Caesar at Philippi, Augustus built a temple to him in the Forum at Rome.

Ulysses
Ulysses, the Latin equivalent of the Greek Odysseus, was the king of Ithaca, a Greek island. He was married to Penelope and they had a son named Telemachus. He was one of the Greek leaders in the Trojan War. The Greeks fought the Trojans for ten years, but Ulysses came up with a plan to burn down Troy and save Helen, the wife of Melanos, the Spartan king. He had the Greek army build a wooden horse that he and nineteen other soldiers could fit in. All of the Greek warships left the shores of Troy and left the horse behind.

The Trojans thought that it was a gift from the Greeks, so the people of Troy brought it through the gates of the city. Late that night, Ulysses and the nineteen soldiers snuck out of the wooden horse and let the newly arrived Greek army through the gates. The

Greeks burned down Troy and saved Helen, but Ulysses still had a long journey ahead of him. Ulysses and his men set sail for Ithaca. After a few weeks of sailing, Ulysses and his men ran out of food. They landed on an island, to look for food and water. They found a whole cave full of food, but they soon found out that the food belonged to a one-eyed giant called a cyclops. Ulysses and his men tricked the cyclops and escaped with the food.

Unfortunately for Ulysses, the cyclops was a son of Neptune, the God of the Sea. Once again, Ulysses' men ran out of food, so they landed on another island. The sailors divided into two groups, Ulysses and some of the crew stayed with the ship, while the others went to look for food. The next morning, one of the "food-searchers" came running back to the boat. The sailor told Ulysses of a sorceress named Circe who had turned the other crew members into hogs. At once, Ulysses ran with the sailor to Circe's palace, but on the way, Mercury came with a gift from one of the gods.

It was a magical flower that would act a shield on Ulysses from Circe's magic. Ulysses met with Circe. Circe tried to use her magic on him, but it didn't work, so she gave in and turned the back into humans. Plus, she warned Ulysses of the dangers to come. With lots of food, Ulysses and his men left the island. Thanks to Circe, Ulysses overcame the next dangers. He overcame the dooming song of the Sirens by plugging the ears of he and his crew.

The sailors came upon the six-headed monster called Scylla. Though all of his crew were eaten by Scylla, Ulysses escaped, only to be washed ashore by a storm where a princess found him and took him to her father. The king gave Ulysses his fastest ship to use to sail home with. When, Ulysses reached Ithaca, he deceived the men that wanted to marry his wife, and killed them. Ulysses finally reclaimed his throne.

Vacuna
A Sabean goddess of agriculture. She was worshipped in a sacred forest near Reate (the current Reati).

Veiovis
Veiovis (Vediovis) is one of the oldest of the Roman gods. He is a

god of healing, and was later associated with the Greek Asclepius. He was mostly worshipped in Rome and Bovillae in Latium. On the Capitoline Hill and on the Tiber Island temples were erected in his honor. In spring, goats were sacrificed to avert plagues. Veiovis is portrayed as a young man, holding a bunch of arrows (or lightning bolts) in his hand, and is accompanied by a goat. He is probably based on the Etruscan god Veive.

Venus
The Roman goddess of love and beauty, but originally a vegetation goddess and patroness of gardens and vineyards. Later, under Greek influence, she was equated with Aphrodite and assumed many of her aspects. Her cult originated from Ardea and Lavinium in Latium. The oldest temple known of Venus dates back to 293 BCE, and was inaugurated on August 18. Later, on this date the Vinalia Rustica was observed. A second festival, that of the Veneralia, was celebrated on April 1 in honor of Venus Verticordia, who later became the protector against vice. Her temple was built in 114 BCE.

After the Roman defeat near Lake Trasum in 215 BCE, a temple was built on the Capitol for Venus Erycina. This temple was officially opened on April 23, and a festival, the Vinalia Priora, was instituted to celebrate the occasion. Venus is the daughter of Jupiter, and some of her lovers include Mars and Vulcan, modeled on the affairs of Aphrodite. Venus' importance rose, and that of her cult, through the influence of several Roman political leaders. The dictator Sulla made her his patroness, and both Julius Caesar and the emperor Augustus named her the ancestor of their (Julian) family: the 'gens Julia' was Aeneas, son of Venus and the mortal Anchises.

Ceasar introduced the cult of Venus Genetrix, the goddess of motherhood and marriage, and built a temple for her in 46 BCE. She was also honored in the temple of Mars Ultor. The last great temple of Venus was built by the emperor Hadrianus near the Coliseum in 135 CE. Roman statues and portraits of Venus are usually identical to the Greek representations of Aphrodite.

Vercvactor
The Roman god of the first ploughing. See also Imporcitor and

Redarator.

Veritas
Veritas ("truth") is the Roman goddess of truth. She is a daughter of Saturn.

Verminus
Verminus ("worm-god") is the Roman god of the worms in cattle.

Vertumnus
The Roman divinity of seasons, changes and ripening of plant life. He is the patron of gardens and fruit trees. He has the power to change himself into various forms, and used this to gain the favor of the goddess Pomona. Vertumnus' cult was introduced in Rome around 300 BCE and a temple was built on the Aventine Hill in 264 BCE. The Vertumnalias, observed on August 13, is his festival. A statue of Vertumnus stood at the Vicus Tuscus.

Vesta
One of the most popular and mysterious goddesses of the Roman pantheon. Vesta is the goddess of the hearth, equated with the Greek Hestia. There is not much known of her origin, except that she was at first only worshipped in Roman homes, a personal cult. Her cult eventually evolved to a state cult. One myth tells that her service was set up by king Numa Pompilius (715-673 BCE). In her temple on the Palatine Hill, the sacred fire of the Roman state burned, which was maintained by the Vestal Virgins.

At the start of the new Roman year, March 1, the fire was renewed. The sacred fire burned until 394 CE. Vesta's temple was situated on the Forum Romanum and was built in the third century BCE. None of her temples, however, contained a statue of the goddess. Her festival is the Vestalia, which was observed from June 7 - 15. On the first day of this festival, the 'penus Vestae', the inner sanctum of the Vesta temple which was kept closed the entire year, was opened for women who came to bring offerings bare-footed. The temple was ritually cleansed on the last day. The ass is Vesta's sacred animal, whose braying supposedly kept the lascivious Priapus away. Vesta is portrayed as a stern woman, wearing a long dress and with her head covered. Her right hand rests against her side and in her left hand she holds a scepter.

Vestius Alonieus
A god who was revered in north-west Hispania. He had a military function and was associated with the bull.

Vica Pota
An ancient Roman goddess of victory. She had a temple at the base of the Velia, Rome.[24]

Victoria
The Roman personification of Victory, worshipped as a goddess, especially by triumphant generals returning from battle. She was held in higher regard by the Romans then her counterpart Nike by the Greeks and when in 382 CE her statue was removed by the emperor Gratianus there was much resistance in the heathen reactionary circles.

Viduus
Viduus ("divider") is the Roman deity who separates soul from the dead body.

Virbius
A minor Roman deity who is mainly mentioned as the consort of Diana. He was worshipped in the sacred forest of Egeria, near Aricia in Latium, and identified with the resurrected Hippolytus.

Viriplaca
The Roman goddess to whom spouses made offering when they had domestic problems.

Virtus
The Roman god of courage and military prowess.

Vitumnus
The Roman god who gave life to the child in the mother's womb.

Volturnus
A river deity associated with the river Volturnus in Campania (Italy), but it could also be an ancient name for the Tiber. The

Volturnalia was observed on August 27.

Volumna
The Roman protective goddess of the nursery.

Vulcan
The Roman god of fire, especially destructive fire, and craftsmanship. His forge is located beneath Mount Etna. It is here that he, together with his helpers, forges weapons for gods and heroes. Vulcanus is closely associated with Bona Dea with whom he shared the Volcanalia, observed on August 23. This festival took place during the height of the Mediterranean drought and the period of highest risk of fire. On the banks of the river Tiber, fires were lighted on which living fish were sacrificed. His temples were usually located outside the cities, due to the dangerous nature of fire.

In 215 BCE his temple on the Circus Flaminius was inaugurated. In Ostia he was the chief god as the protector against fire in the grain storages. He is identified with the Greek Hephaestus.

Vulturnus
The Roman god of the East Wind, equal to the Greek Eurus.

References

1. Micha F. Lindemans, Micha F., Ryan Tuccinardi, Risa Gordon, Mitchell Mendis, James Hunter, and Liz Gunner. Encyclopediae Mythica: Roman Mythology. M.F. Lindemans, Ed. www.pantheon.org. 1995.
2. Virgil I, 550; V, 36, 61, 73. Aeneid V, 525.
3. Virgil I, 188, 312; VI, 34, 158.
4. Livius VII, 6.
5. Thebaid 2.205, 4.32, 9.32
6. Virgil VII, 45, 52, 69, 96.
7. Virgil VII, 47.
8. Livius XXVII, 37,2

9. *Virgil VIII, 630.*
10. *Virgil V, 825.*
11. *Virgil V, 721.*
12. *Virgil I, 292*
13. *Livius I, 5*
14. *Livius I, 3*
15. *Livius X, 1, 9*
16. *Livius XL, 19*
17. *Virgil IV, 288*
18. *Virgil VI, 763*
19. *Virgil V, 838*
20. *Aeneid XI, 785*
21. *Livius I, 12*
22. *Livius X, 36*
23. *Livius I, 9,12[25]*
24. *pantheon.org*

2 PRAYERS TO AESCULAPIUS

Apuleius, Florida 18.38-43

Eius dei hymnum Graeco et Latino carmine uobis ecce <iam> canam [iam] illi a me dedicatum. Sum enim non ignotus illi sacricola nec recens cultor nec ingratus antistes, ac iam et prorsa et uorsa facundia ueneratus sum, (39) ita ut etiam nunc hymnum eius utraque lingua canam, cui dialogum similiter Graecum et Latinum praetexui, in quo sermocinabuntur Safidius Seuerus et Iulius Perseus, (40) uiri et inter se mutuo et uobis et utilitatibus publicis merito amicissimi, doctrina et eloquentia et beniuolentia paribus, incertum, modestia quietiores an industria promptiores an honoribus clariores. (41) Quibus cum sit summa concordia, tamen haec sola aemulatio et in hoc unum certamen est, uter eorum magis Karthagine<m> diligat, atque summis medullitus uiribus contendunt ambo, uincitur neuter. (42) Eorum ego sermonem ratus et uobis auditu gratissimum, mihi compositu congruentem et dedicatu[r] religiosum[mo], in principio libri facio quendam ex his, qui mihi Athenis condidicerunt, percontari a Perseo Graece quae ego pridie in templo Aesculapi disseruerim, (43) paulatimque illis Seuerum adiungo, cui interim Romanae linguae partes dedi. Nam et Perseus, quamuis et ipse optime possit, tamen hodie uobis atticissabit.

Marcus Valerius Martialis, Epigrammata 9.17 To Asculapis

Latona's grandson, revered Aesculapis, by whose mild herbal remedies too briefly are the Fates beguiled, from Rome this child sends You his golden locks, that were once his lord's delight, and along with these the mirror that often assured him he was fair. He hastens to sacrifice these tresses that once circled his shining face, happily to serve, in payment for a vow, if You judge that out of danger he will be. Preserve his youthful grace, though his hair is now shortened, and long may You keep him handsome.

P. Ovidius Naso, Metamorphoses 15.678

"Behold the God!" he cried, "It is the God. Think holy thoughts and walk in reverent silence, all who are present. Oh, most Beautiful, let us behold you to our benefit, and give aid to this people that performs your sacred rites."

P. Terentius Afer, Hecyra 328

I'm sadly afraid Philumena's illness is getting worse. Aesculapius, I do entreat thee, and thee, Salus, that it may not be so.

3 PRAYERS TO APOLLO

Anthologia Latina 2.250.12

Come, O God, kind patron, come! May you favor us in your presence.

Anthologia Latina 2.1841

Phoebus Tirynthia, I pray, please accept this offering on my behalf. This gift I offer in thanks to You for the good health and strength that I have had.

Arnobius Adversus Nationes III 43

Come, Dii Penates, come Apollo and Neptune and all You Gods, and by Your powers may You mercifully turn aside this ill disease that violently twists, scorches and burns our city with fever.

Claudius Claudianus In Olybii et Probini fratres Consules Panegyricus 1-7

O Sol, whose light embraces the world, you orbit inexhaustible, forever returning, your face glowing on each day, your horses harnessed as a team to drive your chariot, with manes braided pleasantly they rise high, passing over rose-red clouds as you rein their frothing fires. Already yet another year begins, measured by the footsteps of brothers, who as new consuls gladly offer their prayers and vows.

Claudius Claudianus In Olybii et Probini fratres Consules Panegyricus 71-2

To you I pray, Apollo of Mount Parnassus, that you may inspire the pythia with so important knowledge, as to whom between us, O God, you will reward with authority.

Corpus Inscriptiones Latinae 141-46; [92-99]: Acta Sacroum Saeculares

Apollo, as it is prescribed for you in those books – and for this reason may every good fortune attend the Roman people, the Quirites – let sacrifice be made to you with nine popana, and nine cakes, and nine phthoes. I beg and pray [that you may increase the sovereign power and majesty of the Roman people, the Quirites, in war and peace; as you have always watched over us among the Latins. Forever may you grant safety, victory and health to the Roman people, the Quirites. May you bestow your favor on the Roman people, the Quirites, and on the legions of the Roman people, the Quirites. May you preserve the health and welfare of the people of Rome, the Quirites, and may you always remain willingly favorable and propitious to the people of Rome, the Quirites, to the college of the quindecimviri, to me, to my house and household. May you accept [this] sacrifice of nine female lambs and nine she-goats, to be burnt whole for you in sacrifice. For these reasons may you be honored and strengthened with the sacrifice of this female lamb, and become favorable and propitious to the Roman people, the Quirites, to the college of the quindecimviri, to myself, to my house, and to my household.] Apollo, just as I have offered popana and prayed to you with proper prayer, for this same reason be honored with these sacrificial cakes. Become favorable and propitious. [Apollo, just as I have offered phthoes cakes and prayed to you with proper prayer, for this same reason be honored with these sacrificial cakes. Become favorable and propitious.

Homeric Hymn to Apollo

XXI. (ll. 1-4) Phoebus, of you even the swan sings with clear voice to the beating of his wings, as he alights upon the bank by the eddying river Peneus; and of you the sweet-tongued minstrel, holding his high-pitched lyre, always sings both first and last. (l. 5) And so hail to you, lord! I seek your favor with my song. (Public Domain - Translated by Evelyn-White)

Horace Carmina 1.31.1-4; 17-20

What may a poet ask in his prayers of You, Apollo? What can he say as he pours a libation of new wine to You? May Apollo grant that I enjoy good health and a sound mind, and, I pray, when I grow old, may He grant me a strife-free life, a clear mind and a lyre beside me with which to sing His praises.

Livy 5.21.2-3:

Pythian Apollo, inspired by You and Your guiding influence I go forth to destroy the city of Veii. A tenth part of its spoils I devote to You. Likewise for You, Juno Regina, who in Veii now dwells, I pray, that after our victory You will follow us to the our City, that soon will become Your City as well, where a holy precinct worthy of Your dignity will be built to receive You.

Martial Epigrammata 4.45.1-2

An offering I gladly give You, Phoebus, a box of fragrant incense, from Palatinus Parthenius on behalf of his son.

Martial Epigrammata 9.42

May Myrina's richness ever You hold, Apollo, thus always the swan song, too, may You enjoy, may the well versed sisters ever serve You, the Delphic Pythia ever reveal any of Your oracles, may the Palatia ever love and revere You. Were You ever to ask, and Caesar grant that he should invest Stella with consular powers, then gladly would I by vow become indebted to You.

Ovid Remedia Amoris 75-6

From the very outset I pray to You, Apollo, inventor of music and of all the healing arts, come to my aid and this undertaking; bless it with Your laurel.

Ovid Remedia Amoris 704

Come, health-bearing Apollo, come favoring my undertaking.

Pacuvius Medus fr. 2

Sol, I call to You that You may guide me on my search for my parents.

Petronius Arbiter 94 PLM

God of Delphi, I have dedicated to You a temple made of fine Sicilian marble, spoken aloud Your praises while accompanied by the sweet sounds of the calamus reeds. If ever You hear our prayers, Apollo, and if indeed You are divine, tell me now, by what means does a man without money seek to find it?

Plautus Aulularia 394-96

Apollo, please, help me, and with your arrows slay these treasure-laden thieves. As you have done before, swiftly come to my aid and draw your bow.

Plautus Mercator 678-80

Apollo, I beseech you, graciously grant peace, prosperity, safety and sound health to our family, and spare my son by your gracious favor.

Sammonicus Praefatio Liber Medicinalis

Phoebus Apollo, bearer of health, for You we compose our song, and favorably promote Your discoveries. With Your healing arts, You lead life back when it is withdrawn from us and recall us from joining the Manes in Heaven. You who formerly dwelt in the temples of Aegea, Pergamum, and Epidaurum, and who drove off the Python from Your peaceful house at Delphi, sought a temple at Rome to Your glory, by expelling the foul presence of illness. Come to me now as each time You have fondly strengthen me when often You were called, and may You be present in all that is set out in this book.

Seneca Hercules Furens 592

Your pardon I do desire, Apollo, if you see in my actions what is forbidden; for it was by the will of another that I revealed hidden things of the earth.

Statius Achilleis 1.9-10

Grant me, O Phoebus, new fonts of inspiration and weave fortune's garland as a crown upon my head.

Statius Thebaid 1.643-5

Not am I sent by anyone, O Apollo of Thymbra, nor as a suppliant do I approach your shrine, conscious of my pious duties and the demands made of me by virtue has led me your way.

Statius Thebaid 1.694-96; 716-18

Pour wine on the altar's fire as we sing our vows again and again to Leto's son, the Preserver of our forefathers.

"Father Phoebus, whether it is the snowy slopes of Lycia or the thorny slopes of Patara that perpetually keep you busy, or if it pleases you to merge your golden hair in Castalia's chaste moisture, ... come now, remembering our hospitality, and bless once more the fertile fields of Juno."

Statius Thebaid 4.694-51

Tell us, O Phoebus, who would have bent their rage, who might cause their delay, and in midcourse turn them astray.

Statius Thebaid 6.296-300

Tell us, O Phoebus, the famous names of their master, tell us the names of the horses themselves. Never before were such swift footed steeds, well-bred and noble, drawn up for battle, just as dense flocks of birds may swiftly clash together or Aeolus decree furious winds to contest on a single shore.

Statius Thebaid 7.786-88

Now my last words before I depart, if any gratitude I owe to your prophet, O Phoebus, I commend my home and family shrines to You, and leave to You the punishment of my faithless wife and my beautiful son's impassioned furor.

Statius Thebaid 8.91-94

O great Surveyor of all men, (Apollo), You who know the causes and principles of our actions, and who is a Father to me and Savior as well, I pray, lessen Your resolve against me and still Your angry heart, do not think me worthy of Your wrath one who is but a man and who fears Your laws.

Statius Thebaid 10.337-45

To You, Phoebus Apollo, go these spoils, prizes of the night, taken from distinguished nobles, not yet washed clean of their blood. I trust that truly I have offered You an acceptable sacrifice. I, Your faithful priest and defender of Your sacred tripod against uncivilized enemies, commit these to You. If I have not disgraced Your traditional rites and strictly kept Your rule, come often to me, think me worthy to often enter into my thoughts and seize my mind. Although now crude honors are offered You, - these broken arms stained with blood of honorable men, - if ever, Paean, You will grant the return of my native home and the temples I long for, God of Lycia, remember my vows, and however many rich gifts and as many bulls as I have promised, demand they be fulfilled.

MEDITATIONS ON THE ROMAN DEITIES

Tibullus 2.5.1-4; 122-3

Give your favor, Phoebus, to a new priest who enters your temple. Be gracious, and with songs and lyre, come! When your fingers pluck the chords, and you give voice to song, I pray you may inspire my words into your praises. May your hair be ever flowing, Phoebus; may your sister be forever chaste.

Tibullus 3.10.1-10; 25-6

Draw near, Apollo, and expel the illness from this tender girl, come, draw near. Phoebus of flowing hair unshorn, hear me and hasten. If, Phoebus, You apply Your healing hand to her, You will not regret saving her. Allow not that she should waste away emaciated, or that her color should wane pallor, or that her limbs should lose their strength, and do not wait until her white limbs turn to a hideous color. Whatsoever this illness may be, whatever sorrow we may fear it will bring, carry it off with the waters of a swift running stream to the seas. Holy one, come! And bring with You all Your delicacies, all Your songs, and all else that will soothe the sick. Then the Gods will raise a pious tumult of Your praises and desire They too had Your healing arts.

Tibullus 4.4.1 ff.

Come, Phoebus, with Your golden hair loosely floating, soothe her torture, restore her fair complexion. Come quickly, we pray, we implore, use Your happy skills, such charms as You never spared before. Grant that her frail fame shall not waste away with consumption, or her eyes grow languid, and her bloom fade. Come now with Your favoring aid.

Valerius Flaccus Argonautica 1.5-7

Advise me, Phoebus Apollo, if ever You inspired the Sibyl of Cumae to see visions waft from a kettle in Your sacred house, if ever a chaplet of fresh laurel dignified a worthy brow, and O You whose great fame opened many a sea.

Valerius Flaccus Argonautica 5.17-20

Turn to us now, Mighty Archer, I pray that finally now, Apollo, You will come to our aid! Father, revive the life of this man. If You approve of what we do, then stir back to life he who is of the utmost importance for the success of our venture; and so from this one does the fate of all hands depends.

Valerius Flaccus Argonautica 5.244-49

The king, startled by his dreams, awoke, arose from his bed and addressed his father, the God of the sun, whose car would soon appear on the eastern shore. "Father Apollo, I pray to You, all-seeing guardian God, be gracious to me and protect me, watching over my kingdom. Be ever vigilant and warn me what strangers or what subjects of mine conspire against me. Whatever treacherous plots there may be, keep me alert and prepared."

Virgil Aeneid 3.85-9

Grant us our own, Lord of Thymbra, grant the tired and worn, and their children, a city behind defensive walls in a tamed land. Safeguard a new Troy, built by those Trojan sons who escaped the Greeks and severe Achilles. Who now must I follow? Where do you urge me to go? Grant, Father, a sign, and flow into our souls.

Virgil Aeneid 6.55-77

O Phoebus Apollo, who always pitied Troy of its grave hardship, you who guided the hand of Paris and his Dardanan missile to the body of Aeacus' son, You who led me to penetrate all the seas that wash upon mighty shores, and deep within the remote Massylian tribes and fields that lie against Syrtian sands, until at last we came upon the fleeting shores of Italy. Let Troy's ill fortune have followed us thus far (and no further). You also may justly spare the families of Pergamus, all you gods and goddesses who stood against Troy and the greater glory of the Dardanians. And You, most holy Diviner of future events, I ask only for what fate has allotted me, grant that the sons of Teucria with their wandering gods and storm tossed spirits of Troy may settle in Latium. Then to Apollo and

Hecate I shall erect a temple in marble and establish feast days celebrated in Apollo's name. For You a great sanctuary also awaits in our new realm, for indeed I shall place within it Your divining lots and record the arcane words Your oracles have spoken to our people, Gracious One, and I will select and consecrate virtuous men to care for them. Do not commit your songs only to the leaves, that they may swirl about as the sport of whirling winds, but sing them, I pray, with your own lips for us.

Virgil Aeneid 10.875-76

Great Father of the Gods may it so come to pass; thus, Apollo, come, make it begin.

Virgil Aeneid 11.785-93

Apollo Soranus, Highest of the Gods, Holy Guardian of Mount Soracte, we who are foremost among Your worshippers, for You we set to flame the piled pine-wood, and Your worshippers, piously trusting our faith in You among the fires, press our step across the glowing embers. Grant, Father Almighty, that by our arms we may erase this disgrace. No plunder did I seek, no trophy to win from virgins, or any spoils; my fame shall follow from my feats. But while this dire plague strikes me with illness, inglorious I must return to the cities of our fathers.

4 PRAYERS TO CERES

Apuleius Metamorphoses 6.2

Then Psyche fell down upon Ceres' feet, sweeping the hard earth with her hair and greatly weeping at Her footsteps, mingled her prayers for forgiveness with claims of her innocence, O merciful Mother, I pray You avert my sorrow, by Your generous and temperate right hand, by the joyful harvest festival, by Your mysteries kept in silent secrecy, by Your winged servants, the dragons who serve Your chariot as You go about, and by the furrows in Sicilian clods of earth, and the plow-wheels that churn them from firm soil, by the marriage of Proserpina that You discovered through diligently seeking after Your daughter, and by the mysteries held in silent secrecy within the Attic temple of Eleusis, halt the misery of Your servant Psyche. Among this piled wheat let me be concealed, if only for a few days, until the ire of so great a Goddess passes, or at least give me a quiet interval that I might rest from my great labour and travail.

Apuleius Metamorphoses 11.2

O blessed Queen of Heaven, whether you are the Lady Ceres who is the original and motherly source of all fruitful things in earth, who after finding Your daughter Proserpina, through the great joy which You did presently conceive, made barren and unfruitful ground to be plowed and sown, and now You inhabit in the land of Eleusis; or whether You are ... Proserpina, by reason of the deadly howling to which You yield, that has power to stop and put away the invasion of the hags and Ghosts which appear unto men, and to keep them down in the closures of the earth; You who is worshipped in divers manners, and does illuminate all the borders of the earth by Your feminine shape, You which nourishes all the fruits of the world by Your vigor and force; with whatsoever name or fashion it is lawful to call upon You, I pray You end my great travail and misery, and deliver me from the wretched fortune, which has for so long a time pursued me. Grant peace and rest if it please You to reply to my entreaties, for I have endured too much labor and peril. Remove from me this misshapen form from me, and return me to my pristine form, and if I have offended in any way the divine Majesty, let me rather die than live, for I am fully weary of my life.

Caesius Bassius Hymn to Ceres and Libera by Philicus

Fertile Goddesses, wives of Jove, may the mystic rite that You cherish not be defiled.

Cato De Agricultura 134

It is fitting to offer the porca praecidanea (to Ceres) prior to the time of reaping. For Ceres offer a sow as Her porca praecidanea before you store these fruits of the earth: spelt, wheat, barley, beans, and the seeds of field mustard. With wine and frankincense pray to Janus, Jupiter and Juno before sacrificing the sow. Offer piled cakes to (Ceres) while saying, "(Ceres Mater), to You I pray with good prayers, offering You this pile of cakes, so that You might willing be favorable to me and my children, to my home and household." ... Afterwards give an offering of wine to (Ceres), "(Ceres Mater), for the same reasons given in the good prayers I prayed while offering You piled cakes, may You accept and be honor by this portion of wine I pour."

Cicero In C. Verrem IV.72. 187-8

O Ceres and Libera, whose sacred worship, as the opinions and religious belief of all men agree, is contained in the most important and most abstruse mysteries; You, by whom the principles of life and food, the examples of laws, customs, humanity, and refinement are said to have been given and distributed to nations and to cities; You, whose sacred rites the Roman people has received from the Greeks and adopted, and now preserves with such religious awe, both publicly and privately, that they seem not to have been introduced from other nations, but rather to have been transmitted from hence to other nations. You, again and again I implore and appeal to, most holy Goddesses, who dwell around those lakes and groves of Enna, and who preside over all Sicily,... You whose invention and gift of corn, which You have distributed over the whole earth, inspires all nations and all races of men with reverence for Your divine power;--And all the other Gods, and all the Goddesses, do I implore and entreat.

Livius Andronicus Equos Troianos

Grant me the strength, Goddess, to whom I ask, to whom I pray; extend your assistance to me.

Da mihi hasce opes, quas peto, quas precor porrige opitula

Livy 24.38.8

Mother Ceres and Proserpina and all You Gods above and below who inhabit the city, these hallowed lakes and groves, I pray that You attend us with Your favor and support, if it should be that we are taking this initial step for the purpose of guarding against treacherous falsehood, not practicing it.

Vos, Ceres Mater ac Proserpina, precor, ceteri superi infernique Di, qui hanc urbem, hoc sacratos lacus locosque colitis, ut ita nobis volentes propitii adsitis, si vitandae, non inferendae fraudis causa hoc consilii capimu.

Ovid Fasti I.671-704: Paganalia Prayer to Ceres and Tellus

O Mothers of Fruitfulness, Earth and Ceres, please, With salted spelt cakes offered for Your mother's woe, In kind service have Earth and Ceres nurtured wheat, She who gave grain life, She who gave us room to grow.

Pray then before the sheep are shorn their winter's fleece.

Consorts in labour who antiquity reformed, Oaken acorn have You replaced by useful meal, With boundless crops satisfy those who fields farmed, O that they may by their tillage their reward seal.

May You grant tender seed abundant increase.

Let not icy cold enwrap our new shoots with snow, While we sow let cloudless skies and fair winds blow.

When the seed lies sprouting, sprinkle with gentle rains, May You ward off the feasting by birds from our grains.

You also, little ants, spare the grain we have sown, More abundant will be your harvest when 'tis grown. Meanwhile may our grain not blight by rough mildew, Nor foul weather our seed blanch to a sickly hue.

Never may our grain be shriveled nor may it swell, Without eye-stinging cockle, not by wild oats held.

Crops of wheat, of barley, of spelt grow on the farm, Look now, Good Mothers, guard well the field, The seasons change, the earth by Your breath grows warm, With Your gentle touch may You increase our yield.

By Peace Ceres nursed, Her foster-child live in peace.

Ovid Amores III 10. 3-14; 43-8

Flaxen haired Ceres, Your fine tresses wreathed with ears of wheat, why must your sacred rites inhibit our pleasures? Goddess, people everywhere praise for your munificence. No other goddess so lavishes men and women with everything good. In earlier times the uncouth peasant never roasted grains of wheat, never knew a threshing floor, but oak trees, those first oracles, provided them with gruel. Acorns, tender roots and herbs made their meal then. Ceres first taught seeds to ripen in the fields, taught how to follow Her with scythe against their golden hair, first broke the oxen to yoke and reveal the fertile earth beneath its curved blade.

O golden haired Ceres, just because lying apart was so sad for You. must I now, too, suffer so on Your holy day? Why must I be sad when You rejoice at the return of Your daughter whose realm is the lesser only to Juno's? A festival calls for singing and drinking and lovemaking. These are fit gifts to carry to the temples and please the gods.

Ovid, Ibis 419-20

May the son of Ceres be forever sought by you in vain; and may you always remain destitute, your prayers for wealth and fortune frustrated by Him.

Seneca, Hercules Furens 229

For you, Goddess of the Fruits of the Earth, your secret rites I will fund; in your shrine at Eleusius shall burn the sacred flame in celebration of your mysteries.

Servius Honoratus, On the Georgics 1.21

Fabius Pictor enumerates these lesser gods, who the flamen Cerealis invokes when offering sacrifice to Tellus and Ceres: Vervactor, Reparator, Imporcitor, Insitor, Obarator, Occator, Sarritor, Subruncinator, Messor, Convector, Conditor, and Promitor.

Tibullus I.1.15-6

Golden-haired Ceres, bless this our farm; a crown of wheat I shall hang before your altar.

Tibullus II.1.3-4; 17-20

Come to us, Bacchus, with clusters of grapes dangling from your horns, and you, too, Ceres, a wreath of newly ripened wheat for your temples, come!

Gods of our fathers, we purify our farmers and our fruitful fields; we ask that you drive away harm from our borders. Let not the now sprouting plants succumb before harvest, let not the timid lambs be outrun by swift wolves.

Virgil Georgics I.7-12:

Liber and gentle Ceres, if by your gifts the earth once changed, exchanging Chaonian acorns for rich heads of grain, and receiving your invention of wine from Acheloian cups, and you Fauns, your divine presence an aid for rustics, bring dancing feet, as when Dryad girls frolic with Fauns, of your gifts I sing.

5 PRAYERS TO DII INFERI

Faunus

Horace Carmen 3.8.1-8

Amorous Faunus, from whom the Nymphs flee, step lightly across my boundaries and sunny fields, and soon depart, leaving your blessing on my young lambs and kids, and leveled tender shoots.

If gentle, at year's end a plumb kid I'll offer, with wine libations liberally poured from the cups of Venus' devotees, and many sweet, fragrant herbs I'll burn on your ancient altar.

Virgil Aeneid 12.777-9

Faunus, have pity, I pray, and you, opulent Earth, hold fast this weapon, if always I have honored your worship in good faith.

Hecate

Virgil Aeneid 4.609-12

Nocturnal Hecate, who is called at the crossroads throughout the City, and Avenging Dirae, and Elissa's gods of the dying, hear our prayers, heed them, and direct your awful powers against those who deserve it.

Pales

Ovid Fasti 4.747

Pray to Pales with warm milk, say: Be equally mindful of sheep and their masters, Pales. May my stables escape from harm. If I have grazed my flock in sacred pastures, or sat beneath a sacred tree, if unknowingly my sheep plunked their fodder from gravesites, if I have entered a sacred grove forbidden to men, and the nymphs and the half goat gods fled in fear at the sight of me, if my knife has pruned a shady bough to give a basket of leaves to an ailing sheep, grant indulgence of my offenses. Do not fault me for sheltering my herd in your sacred shrines when it was hailing heavily. Do not harm me for disturbing your pools; O Nymphs, pardon me for stirring up the riverbeds, the hooves of my flock turning your clear waters muddy. Goddess, may you placate for us the spirits of springs and fountains, and placate the freckles gods of every grove. Keep us from seeing the Dryads and Diana at Her bath, and the Fauns lying out in pastures at midday. Repel illness far away from us. Grant health to herds and men, and to the vigilant pack of guard dogs. May I never herd home less than were counted in the morning. May I never bewail the torn fleece of my sheep carried off by a wolf. May unjust famine remain.

Virgil Georgics 3.1-2

Also you, great Pales, in memory of you we sing, shepherd of Amphrysis, and all of you who come from forests and streams on mount Lycaeus in Arcadia.

Priapus

Petronius Satyricon 133

Companion of Nymphs, companion of Bacchus, Priapus, Whom Dione appointed God of lush forests, honored in Lesbos and verdant Thasos, worshipped by the Lydians whose land is crossed by seven rivers and who built a temple to You in Your Hypaepan homeland, come to me, protector of Bacchus, beloved of Dryads, and hear my humble prayers. +++ My prayer is this: Relieve me of a guilty conscious, forgive my venial offense and when Fortuna next smiles on me, praises and thanksgiving I shall offer You. A goat with gilt horns, the finest of his herd, I shall bring to Your altars. The suckling piglet of a sow I shall bring to Your altars. Foaming new wine, borne by young men I shall bring to Your altars. All these offering in procession shall I order to pass three times around Your shrine.

Tibullus 1.1.17-18

Red guardian, Priapus, placed within this fruitful garden, with your fierce scythe frighten off the birds from this crop.

Tibullus 1.4.1-6

May leafy shade shelter you, Priapus, and neither the hot sun nor snowy storms bring you harm. By what ingenuity or skill do you seize beauties? Certainly not by gleaming beard, nor with stylish hair, as naked you pass through the icy winds of winter, and naked still beneath the Dogstar you remain through the parching sun of summer.

Virgil Eclogues 7.33-36

Priapus, a large cup of milk and this libum bread is all you can expect each year, guardian of a pauper's garden. For a while yet your image is carved in stone, but if at breeding time you make good the herds, then of gold your image we shall make.

Robigo

Ovid Fasti 4.911-32

Spare Ceres' grain, O scabby Robigo, let the tips of sprouting shoots gently quiver above rich soil. Let the crops grow, nurtured in turn as each star passes through the heavens, until full and ripe they are readied for the scythe. Your power is not light. What grain You touch, the farmer notes as lost. Wind and rain damage Ceres' grain enough, And by glistening white snow is burnt. Worst still if the stalks are damp when the Titan sears them, Your season of anger, fearful Goddess, when Sirius rises with the sun, Spare them, I pray. Away with scabrous hands from the harvest Do not harm the cultivated fields. The power to harm is enough. May You not grasp the crops, but embrace hard iron. Destroy first whatever else is able to destroy. Better to seize the destructive spear and sword, for they have no use, when the world puts forth quiet peace. Now may glimmer the light hoes and rough two-pronged hoes and let the arcing plow shine, polished from rural work. Corrupt iron weapons instead with Your rust And may any impulse to draw sword be thwarted by sheaths rusted from long neglect. Do not violate Ceres, but allow the farmer time to fulfill his vows for Your absence.

Terminus

Ovid Fasti 2.658-62; 2.673-8

Holy Terminus, You define people and cities and nations within their boundaries. All land would be in dispute if without You. You seek no offices or anyone's favor; no amount of gold can corrupt Your judgment. In good faith You preserve the legitimate claims to rural lands.

Terminus, You have lost Your freedom to move about, remain on guard, positioned where You were stationed, never to concede whatever claims a neighbor may make, lest You would appear to give an upper hand to men over vows witnessed by Jupiter, and whether ploughshares or mattocks give You a beating, proclaim, "Yours is this land, that is his.

6 PRAYERS TO DIANA

Apuleius Metamorphosis XI.2: Lucius' Prayer for the Assistance of Isis

Diana, who are the sister of the God Phoebus, who nourishes so many people by the generation of beasts, and are now adored at the sacred places of Ephesus, ... You who is worshipped in divers manners, and does illuminate all the borders of the earth by Your feminine shape, You which nourishes all the fruits of the world by Your vigor and force; with whatsoever name or fashion it is lawful to call upon You, I pray You end my great travail and misery, and deliver me from the wretched fortune, which has for so long a time pursued me. Grant peace and rest if it please You to reply to my entreaties, for I have endured too much labor and peril.

Catullus 34.5:

Diana, in faith, we are pure girls and boys, allow us to sing to You. Diana, magnificent child of still greater Jove, whose mother Latona gave You birth in an olive grove on Delos. Lady of the Mountains who runs over hills and through dark forests, over the wild rough hill country and through the tall grass of hidden valleys, in mountain pastures cut by roaring streams. Women in the pain of childbirth call you Lucina. You are Trivia, goddess of witches. You are Luna, the luminous moon. Monthly is measured the progress of Your journey through the year while You fill the rustic homes of good farmers with the fruits of the earth. By whatsoever holy name it pleases You, from antiquity have You accepted our customary offerings, preserve in good faith the children of Romulus as ever You graced our ancestors.

Corpus Inscriptiones Latinae III suppl. 8298

Virgin Goddess of Delia, known for Your favoring grace, what offerings You demand I happily give.

Corpus Inscriptiones Latinae X.3796

Resident of Tifata, Glorious Virgin of hunters, in this place, Daughter of Latona, was Your temple established, renowned by the whole of mankind, Dweller of the Forest, and here as well, an unending praise of life for You who preserves honor. ...Before were born the hills or the forests, She unfolds so much from the clouds of the mind.

Grattius Faliscus Cynegetica 1-2

I sing in thanks for the gifts of the Gods, and for those gifts, O Diana, which are under Your auspices, for those skills in which hunters delight.

Horace Carmina I.21.1; 5-8

Tender virgins recite their prayers to You, Diana, You who delight in dark rivers and quivering forest foliage, wherever You may be, atop the chilly height of Algidus, or in the Erymanthic woods, or verdant Cragus.

Horace Carmina III.22.1-8

Guardian of hills and forest groves, Virgin, whom young mothers thrice invoke at childbirth, listen and deliver them from death. Triple goddess, to You I dedicate this pine tree that now overhangs my villa and each year the blood of a wild boar, who ponders an oblique thrust, I will gladly give to its roots as drink.

Horace Carmen Saeculares lines 1-4; 13-16; 69-72

O shining Phoebe and forest Diana, Lucidum, shining ornaments of the sky, ever gentle and refined, O sacred brows, give us what we pray for now.

Gentle Moon, Ilithyia, Lucina, by whatever name you wish to be called, Gentalis, watch over mothers, may You give them gentle deliveries.

Diana, who dwells on the Aventine and Algidus hilltops, graciously lend Your ears to the prayers of virile men and young boys.

Laevius FPR fr. 26; p. 292:

Therefore adoring You as though You were nurturing Venus Herself, whether You are female, or whether You are male, even so, Illuminating the Night, You are a nurturing Moon.

Livius Andronicus Equos Troianos:

Grant me the strength, Goddess, to whom I ask, to whom I pray; extend Your assistance to me.

Ovid Amores II 14.19-24

Ilithyia, You who are compassionate towards women in labor, who suffer with great pains in their womb, their bodies strained in slow birth of the hidden child, gently attend to her, Ilithyia, and favor my prayers. She is worthy of Your aid, reward her with life, I will myself, dressed in pure white robes offer frankincense upon Your altar, I will myself carry votive gifts to lay at Your feet. And to Your altar's inscription I shall add, "By Naso, for Corinna saved." Act in this manner, and receive the legend inscribed and the gifts in Your sanctuary.

Ovid Fasti II 449-52

Thanks be to You, Lucina, who are named for this sacred grove, or else because it is You, Goddess, who brings life into the light of day. Kind Lucina, I pray that You spare pregnant girls from labor's hardship, and gently birth ripened infants from their wombs.

Ovid Fasti III 255-6

(Diana) Lucina, You have given us light, attend our birthing prayers.

Ovid Metamorphoses I.487-9

Daphne, daughter of Peneus pleaded, Father, grant me what Diana's father has granted Her; let me remain, as I am, a woman, virgin and free.

Ovid Metamorphoses V.618-20

Help me, Diana, for I am overwhelmed. Diana, I am Your servant, Your arms-bearer, to whom You have often given Your bow to carry, and who filled Your quiver with arrows.

Ovid Metamorphoses VI.327-8

Favour me, Goddess, lead me, and lend me your support.

Servius Honoratus Ad Aeneis 1.330

Whoever you may be, whether Diana or a Nymph, may You favor us and lighten our labors.

Silius Italicus Punica Liber XIII. 13.137:

Come favorably, Diana, daughter of Latona, onto our undertaking.

Statius Thebaid IV 746-64;

Potent Goddess of sacred groves - for by your noble appearance and modesty I think You are not born of mortals - beneath a starry sky delighting, no need have you to search for water; come quickly then to help your neighbors. Whether Diana, who is mighty with the bow and Latona's daughter, has sent you from Her chaste company to the bridal chamber, or whether a lapse for humble love has drawn you from the stars above to make you fertile, for the Arbiter among the Gods is Himself not new to Argive wedding beds, look with favor upon a tired army on the march. We determined that Thebes deserves to be destroyed with the sword brought forward, but now severe drought makes us no longer war-like, it bends our hearts, ands weakens us into idleness. Grant drink to those who are weary, whether you hold a babbling brook or stagnant pool. This will bring no shame or desecration to your place. Winds, you now are asked along with Jove for rain, may you refresh our virile and bellicose hearts and replenish our lifeless spirits. Thus with favoring skies may this burden to you thrive with rain laden clouds. Only Jupiter may grant that we will return with plunder, but if so, O Goddess, war gained riches we will pile as offerings of thanks to you. For your sanctuary, Goddess, a great altar we will build, and wash it in the blood of numerous Boeotian cattle to repay your kindness.

Statius Thebaid VI 633-37

Goddess, divine power of woodland groves, to You and to Your honor, these locks of my hair are owed, and by the vow made to You also comes this wrong. If my mother or I merited your good assistance in the hunt, I ask You not allow me to go to Thebes under foreboding signs, nor allow Arcadia to plunge into so much shame.

Statius Thebaid IX 608-35

Virgin Goddess of the sacred groves, whose unkind banners and fierce battle cries I follow, scorning my sex in a manner unlike the Greeks. Not the throngs in Colchis or the assembled Amazons cherish Your sacred rites more than I. If ever did I not boldly enter Bacchic revelries of the night and, although disgraced unseen in the bedroom, nevertheless I did not bear with joy the smooth shaft of the thyrsus or the soft sacks, and even after I married, though my virgin purity was soiled, in my heart of hearts I remained a virgin huntress. I took no care to hide my fault from You in some secret cave, but held out my son to You, confessed my shame and trembling laid him at Your feet. He was not of degenerate blood, not weak or mild, but straightaway he crawled to my bow and as a babe cried for my arrow. For him I pray – whose fate causes me these restless nights and threatening dreams – for him, who now audaciously goes too boldly off to war, I pray to You that I may see him victorious, or, if I pray for too much, grant at least that I may see him once more. In this let him perspire and bear Your arms. Suppress the ill-boding omens. What foreign Maenades, what Theban gods, I ask You, Diana of the sacred Delian grove, hold power in our forest? Leave me! Deep within my heart – may the augury be in vain – why, deep within my heart, do I see such dire omens in this mighty oak? If what worrisome dreams are sent me in my sleep truly presage the future, I pray, merciful Dictynna, by Your mother's labors and Your brother's glory, with all Your arrows pierce deeply this unhappy womb, and let him first hear of his wretched mother's death.

Statius Thebaid X 360-70

By these wandering stars I swear, by the shade of my leader, who is to me a divine power, that like the depth of my grief so is my deep resolve. Once my mind was downcast in mournful search of my friend, but now I shall lead the way, Cynthia, mistress of arcane mysteries of the night. If Your divine power, as they assert, is threefold and You descend into the forest each time with a different appearance, it was he who recently was Your companion, and whose honor was nurtured in Your sacred grove. At least consider now to lend me Your aid, for it is this boy, Diana, for whom I search.

Terentius Andria 232

I pray, You Gods, grant an easy delivery to this girl, and assign to someone else the ill fate that awaits the day when the midwife makes her mistakes.

Tibullus IV.iv.1 sqq.

Come, Phoebus, with Your golden hair loosely floating, soothe her torture, restore her fair complexion. Come quickly, we pray, we implore, use Your happy skills, such charms as You never spared before. Grant that her frail fame shall not waste away with consumption, or her eyes grow languid, and her bloom fade. Come now with Your favoring aid.

Tibullus IV.vi.1 sqq

Come, most chaste Queen of Heaven, appear in royal robes and nod Your assent to the wine that is poured and the cakes piled high to await You. With You bring every herb for ending pain, and soothing songs to sing; across the ocean from distant shores bear such herbs as will cure our most severe ills, or whatever else we most fear. Rack this girl no more with pain, or cruelly delay her birthing.

Valerius Cato Lydia 41-44

Your love, O Moon, is with You; why then am I not also with mine? O Moon, You know what grief is; pity one who grieves. (Endymion) who caresses You, O Phoebus, celebrates love with a laurel, and what procession has not told the story to the Gods, or when has fame not told it to the forest?

Virgil Aeneid IX.404-5

You, O divine daughter of Latona, Glory of the Stars and Guardian of the Sacred Groves, be present, Diana, that You may succor us who labor.

Virgil Aeneid XI.583-85

(Diana), skillful in arms, leader in battle and guardian of soldiers, with Your hand, Tritonian Virgin, shatter the spear of this Phrygian pirate; throw him to the ground and stretch him out prostrate beneath our high gate.

Virgil Aeneid XI.557-60

Gracious (Diana), virgin daughter of Latona, who inhabits sacred groves and nurtures woodlands, I, her father, vow this child into service as Your handmaiden. Holding Your weapons before all others, Your supplicant flees on the wind from the enemy. Bear witness to my vow, I pray, O Goddess, and accept her as Your own, whom I now commit to a precarious breeze.

Virgil Eclogues 4.8-10

Only do You, at the boy's birth, in whom a golden race now arises the world over, and the men of iron first begin to pass away, You alone favor him, chaste Lucina; indeed Your own Apollo reigns.

7 PRAYERS TO HERCULES

Anonymous Elegy to Maecenus 1.57-68

O Hercules, energetic Alcidean, unwearied after so many labors, so they recall, even so You laid aside Your cares and made delightful play with a tender girl, having forgotten the Nemean lion, and also the Erymanthian boar. What should come afterward? Twisting spindles with Your thumbs, biting smooth the rough threads in Your mouth. Lydian Omphale beat you for repeatedly knotting and breaking the thread with Your rough hands. Often she would lead You as one of her spinning maidens dressed in flowing robes. Your knotty club together with the lion's skin was thrown down to the ground, and Amor danced upon them with light feet. Who would have thought that would come about when as a babe You strangled monstrous serpents with hands that could barely grasp, or when You swiftly cut off the heads of the Hydra as each grew back again? or conquered the savage steeds of Diomede, or when alone You fought the three brothers who shared a common body and contended with six hands? After the Lord of Olympus routed the sons of Aloeus they say He rested on a bed until the bright of day, and then sent His eagle in search and bring back anyone worthy to lovingly serve Jove, until in an Idaean valley he found You, handsome priest, and gently carried You away in his talons.

L. Apuleius Madaurensis, Metamorphoses sive Asinus aureus 9.21

dignus hercules, dignus, qui et ista vincula conteras et insuper carceris etiam tenebras perferas.

Fittingly, by Hercules, fittingly, if you let the time pass in patience, your bonds, your imprisonment also you may endure.

Corpus Inscriptiones Latinae I 1290

Lucius Aufidius, son of Decius, deservedly devotes this gift to you, Hercules, to pay an annual tithe (for the upkeep of your shrine). At the same time he asks of You, You who are a holy God, to help him and give him Your peace.

Corpus Inscriptiones Latinae VI 312

Te precor Alcide sacris / Invicte peractis / rite tuis laetus dona / ferens meritis / haec tibi nostra potest / tenuis perferre camena / nam grates dignas tu / potes efficere / sume libens simulacra / tuis quae munera Cilo / aris urbanus dedicat / ipse sacris

Corpus Inscriptiones Latinae VI 319

Argive Hercules Victor, to you the urban praetor Veldumnianus Iunius offers a gift in this place.

P. Horatius Flaccus, Sermones 2.6

Oh that some accident would discover to me an urn [full] of money! as it did to him, who having found a treasure, bought that very ground he before tilled in the capacity of an hired servant, enriched by Hercules' being his friend. if what I have at present satisfies me grateful, I supplicate you with this prayer: make my cattle fat for the use of their master, and everything else, except my genius:3 and, as you are wont, be present as my chief guardian. Wherefore, when I have removed myself from the city to the mountains and my castle, (what can I polish, preferably to my satires and prosaic muse?) neither evil ambition destroys me, nor the heavy south wind, nor the sickly autumn, the gain of baleful Libitina.

P. Ovidius Naso, Metamorphoses 15.39-40

O Hercules, to whom twelve labors was given, help me, I pray, since you are witness to the accusations made against me.

Aulus Persius Flaccus, Satura 2.10-15

'o si sub rastro crepet argenti mihi seria dextro Hercule! pupillumue utinam, quem proximus heres inpello, expungam; nam et est scabiosus et acri bile tumet. Nerio iam tertia conditur uxor.'

T. Maccius Plautus, Asinaria 467

By Hercules, may all the gods damn him.

T. Maccius Plautus, Curculio 358

Be silent a while. He threw a most losing cast. I took up the dice, and invoked Hercules as my genial patron; I threw a first-rate cast, and pledged him in a bumping cup; in return he drank it off, reclined his head, and fell fast asleep. I slyly took away from him the ring, and took my legs quietly from off the couch, so that the Captain mightn't perceive it. The servants enquired whither I was going; I said that I was going whither persons when full are wont to go. When I beheld the door, at once on the instant I took myself away from the place.

[Most losing cast: When playing with the "tali," or "knucklebone dice," with only four marked sides, they used sets of four. "Volturii quatuor" (literally, "the four vultures") was the most unlucky throw of all, and is supposed to have been four ones. The first-rate cast: The best throw with the "tali" was called "Venus" or "Venereus jactus," when the dice turned up 2, 3, 4, and 5. As it was by this throw that the Romans chose the King of the Feast, it received the name of "Basilicus," "the king's throw."]

T. Maccius Plautus, Bacchides 892

So may Jupiter, Juno, Ceres, Minerva, Spes, Latona, Ops, Virtus, Venus, Castor, Pollux, Mars, Mercury, Hercules, Summanus; the Sun, Saturn, and all the Deities, prosper me, he neither reclines with her, nor walks, nor kisses, nor does that which is wont to be reported.

Propertius Eligiae 4.9.71-4

Because Your hands have purified the Earth, the Sabines of Cures called You Sancus, The Holy One. Hail Father Sancus, whom austere Juno now favors. O Sancus, may You wish to be with me and Your spirit be in my books.

Silius Italicus Punica 1.505-7

Hercules, Founder of our city (Saguntum), you who are called Alcidus, in whose footsteps we now reside on this hallowed earth, avert the threatening storms from our land.

Statius Silvae 3.1.23-28

Come hither, Hercules, who, now free of your obligations, may choose whether to live in your native Argos and spurn death as Eurystheus buried in his tomb, or whether your virtue has won you a place among the stars beneath the throne of your father Jupiter, and Hebe, better than Phrygian Ganymede, with her robe girded, offers you a cup of blessed nectar to drink, come hither, and grace this newly dedicated temple with the presence of your genius.

Statius Silvae 3.1.154-58

Why not arouse yourself, Hercules, to come and to graciously honor these feats of the festival we hold in your name; whether to split the clouds with your discus, or send your javelin speeding more swiftly than Zephyrs, or whether it please you to lock arms in a Libyan wrestling competition, indulge our ceremonies with your divine presence.

Virgil Aeneid 8.301-2

Hail, Hercules, true son of Jove, an added Glory for the Gods are you. Come now, and dance at your holy rites with skillful feet.

8 PRAYERS TO ISIS

Aretalogy of Isis from Cyme ~translation by Fredrick C. Grant

The aretalogy of Isis, found at Cyme, was written in Greek during the second century c.e. Included in the inscription was a claim to its having been copied from a stele at Memphis. Although reference may have been given to Egypt as the homeland of Isis, the ideas expressed here are derived from the Greek cult of Serapis. In style and conception, it is quite different than is found among the literature of Pharaonic Egypt. Several such aretalogies of Isis are known from other sites, and compare with the epiphany of Isis found in Book 11 of The Golden Ass by Apuleius, written around the same time.

I am Isis, the mistress of every land, and I was taught by Hermes, and with Hermes I devised letter, both the sacred and the demotic, that all might not be written with the same letters:

I gave and ordained laws for all men and women, which no one is able to change. I am the eldest daughter of Kronos. I am the wife and sister of King Osiris. I am She who findeth fruit for men and women I am the Mother of King Horus. I am She that riseth in the Dog Star. I am she that is called goddess by women. For me was the city of Bubastis built. I divided the earth from the heavens. I showed the paths of the stars. I ordered the course of the sun and moon. I devised business in the sea. I made strong the right. I brought together man and woman. I appointed women to bring their infants to birth in the tenth lunar month. I ordained that parents should be loved by children. I laid punishment upon those disposed without natural affection towards their parents. I made with my brother Osiris an end to the eating of human flesh. I revealed mysteries unto men. I taught men and women to honor the images of the gods. I consecrated the precincts of the gods. I broke down the governments of tyrants. I made an end to murders. I compelled women to be loved by men. I made the right to be stronger than gold and silver. I ordained that the true should be thought good. I devised marriage contracts. I assigned to Greeks and to barbarians their languages. I made the beautiful and the shameful to be distinguished by nature. I ordained that nothing should be more feared than an oath. I have delivered the plotter of evil against other men into the hands of the one he plotted against. I established penalties for those who practice injustice. I decree mercy to suppliants. I protect and honor righteous guards. With me the right prevails.

I am the Queen of rivers and winds and sea. No one is held in honor without my knowing it. I am Queen of War. I am Queen of the Thunderbolt. I stir up the sea and I calm it once again. I am in the rays of the sun. Whatever I please, this too shall come to an end. With me everything is reasonable. I set free those in bonds. I am the Queen of seamanship. I make the navigable unnavigable when it pleases me. I create walls for cities. I am called the Lawgiver. I brought up islands out of the depths into the light. I am Lord of Rainstorms. I overcome Fate. Fate hearkens to me. Hail, O Egypt, that nourished me!

Apuleius The Golden Ass 11.2: Lucius' Prayer for the Assistance of Isis

O blessed Queen of Heaven, whether you are the Lady Ceres who is the original and motherly source of all fruitful things in earth, who after finding Your daughter Proserpina, through the great joy which

You did presently conceive, made barren and unfruitful ground to be plowed and sown, and now You inhabit in the land of Eleusis; or whether You are the celestial Venus, who in the beginning of the world did couple together all kind of things with an engendered love, by an eternal propagation of human kind, are now worshipped within the Temples of the Isle Paphos, You, Diana, who are the sister of the God Phoebus, who nourishes so many people by the generation of beasts, and are now adored at the sacred places of Ephesus, You who is Proserpina, by reason of the deadly howling to which You yield, that has power to stop and put away the invasion of the hags and Ghosts which appear unto men, and to keep them down in the closures of the earth; You who is worshipped in divers manners, and does illuminate all the borders of the earth by Your feminine shape, You which nourishes all the fruits of the world by Your vigor and force; with whatsoever name or fashion it is lawful to call upon You, I pray You end my great travail and misery, and deliver me from the wretched fortune, which has for so long a time pursued me. Grant peace and rest if it please You to reply to my entreaties, for I have endured too much labor and peril. Remove from me this shape of mine as an ass, and return me to my pristine form, and if I have offended in any way the divine Majesty, let me rather die than live, for I am fully weary of my life.

Apuleius The Golden Ass 11.5: The Aretalogy of Isis

Behold Lucius, moved by your weeping and prayers, I am come to succor you. I am She that is the natural mother of all life, mistress of all the Elements, the first child of time, supreme deity, chief among powers divine, the Queen of Heaven! I am the principal of the celestial Gods, the light of Goddesses, and the uniform manifestation of all gods and goddesses: I am who governs by my nod the crests of light in the sky. At my will are the planets of the air, the wholesome wafts upon the Seas, and the lamentable silences below disposed. My name, my divinity is venerated throughout all the world in divers manners, in variable rites and in many names. Thus the Phrygians call me Pessinuntia, Mother of the Gods. The Athenians call me Cecropian Minerva. The Cyprians, in their isle home call me Paphian Venus. The Cretan archers call me Diana Dictynna. The three-tongue Sicilians call me Stygian Proserpina. The Eleusians call me the ancient goddess Ceres. Some call me Juno, by others, Bellona, still others Hecate, while some call me Rhamnusia. But those who are enlightened by the earliest rays of that divine sun, principally the Ethiopians which dwell in the Orient, and the Egyptians which are excellent in all kind of ancient lore, and by proper ceremonies are they accustomed to worship me, do call me Queen Isis. I am present; I am with pity; I have come propitiously to favor you during your misery. Shed your tears; indeed, let go your sorrows and put away your mourning. And in a moment, by my foresight, I will enclose your days with wholesome health and beneficial wealth. Therefore from this day on, direct your troubled thoughts to my commands alone. This day, and whichever days shall be born from this night hence, forever, when you call upon my name with reverence, to calm the tempests of winter and smooth stormy seas of choppy waves, opening them to navigation, indeed to the passages across rough open seas, my priest shall henceforth dedicate songs and pour libations. That sacred rite you must never delay nor wait upon knowing it may profane.

Apuleius The Golden Ass 11.25: Lucius' Prayer of Thanks

Most holy and everlasting, blessed Lady, Redeemer and perpetual comfort of human kind, who by Your bounty and grace nourish all the world, cherish our lives, and bestow the consoling smiles of a Mother with great affection upon our trials and tribulations. As a loving Mother You take no rest. There is no day or night, not so much as a moment, that is not filled by Your mercy succoring all men and women. On land as well as at sea, You are She who chases away all storms and dangers from our lives by Your right hand. Likewise You restrain the fatal dispositions, appease the great tempests of fortune and keep back the course of the stars. The Gods supernal do honor You. The Gods of the earth hold You in reverence. You rotate the globe. You give light to the Sun. You govern the world in time and space. You tread down the powers of Hades. By You the seasons return, the Planets rejoice, the Elements serve. At Your command the winds do blow, the clouds do gather, the seeds prosper, and the fruits prevail. The birds of the air, the beasts of the hill, the serpents of the den, and the fish of the sea, do tremble at Your majesty. O but my spirit is not able to give You sufficient praise, nor have I the means to offer You acceptable sacrifice. My voice has no power to utter what I think of You. Not if I had a thousand mouths and so many tongues, not in an eternal flow of unwearied declaration could I affirm it. Howbeit, poor as I am, I shall do as a good religious person, and according to my means, I shall always keep a remembrance of Your countenance deep within my breast, and there in the secret depths of my souls shall I keep divinity forever guarded.

Tibullus 1.3.27-8

Help me now, Isis! Give succor to me beneath your breast. I've seen, drawn on the walls of your temple, the many pictures of your worshippers who have received your aid.

Tibullus 1.7.43-54; 63-4

Somber cares and lamentations, Osiris, were never part of your realm, but song and dance and joyfulness you love. Copious flowers and clusters of ivy berries crown our forehead; yellow skirts and robes of Tyrian purple swirl about the tender feet and limbs of those who dance around your vase of sacred objects to the sound of sweet music. Come celebrate in the spirit of these games, in the spirit of these dances, in the joyous spirit of this temple, where many times pure libations are poured in your honor. Allow us to present you with the sweet scents of glistening ointments to drip upon your hair, garlands of flowers to place upon your head and soft neck. Come, Osiris, that we may present you with incense, and cakes sweetened with Grecian honey. Come, gentle Osiris, to this annual celebration of your birth, O ever bright, ever shining spirit, come!

Ovid Amores 2.13.7-18

O Isis, who dwells in Paraetonium and the genial fields of Canopus, in Memphis and palm-rich Pharos, and where the broad Nile swiftly disgorges into the salty sea through seven mouths, may Osiris always love your pious rites, may the serpent ever glide slowly nearby to bless Your altar gifts, and the horned Apis ever walk beside You in procession. Come hither, by a mere expression of

Your eyes summon, and in one motion save us both, for You will grant life to my lady, and she to me.

9 PRAYERS TO JANUS

Ausonius 3.5

Janus, come! The New Year is here, come and renew the sun.

Cato De Agricultura 134

Father Janus, to You I pray with good prayers, offering You this pile of cakes, so that You might willing be favorable to me and my children, to my home and household.

Father Janus, for the same reasons given in the good prayers I prayed while offering You piled cakes, may You accept and be honor by this portion of wine I pour.

Festus s. v. Chaos

Janus, who was before all the Gods, to whom our parents first invoked in their prayers, from whom all things proceed.

Horace Satires 2.6.20-21

Father Matutinus, or else Janus, if You so prefer to hear, regarded by men as the beginning of works and life's labors, so does it please the Gods, may You begin my song.

Livy 1.32.10

Hear, o Jupiter, and You Janus Quirinus, and all You heavenly Gods, and You gods of earth and of the lower world, hear me! I call You to witness that this people is unjust and does not fulfill its sacred obligations.

Livy 8.9.6

Janus, Jupiter, Mars Pater, Quirinus, Bellona, Lares, Divi Novensiles, Di Indigetes, Gods who have power over us and our enemies, and You Manes, to You I pray, I venerate, I ask Your divine favor and beseech You, that You prosper the virtuous might and victory of the Roman People, the Quirites, and upon the enemies of the Roman People, the Quirites, may You afflict them with terror, fear, and death. As I have pronounced the words, even so on behalf of the Republic of the Roman People, the Quirites, and of the Army, the legions and the auxiliaries of the Roman People, the Quirites, do I devote myself and with me the legions and auxiliaries of our enemies to the gods of the Underworld and to Mother Earth.

Martial Epigrammata 8.2.8

May You give, Father Janus, what we ask of You.

Martial Epigrammata 8.8.1-6

Janus, though You begin each fleeting year, and renew the long ages wherever You appear, though vows and incense are piously first offered to You, and the consuls begin each year by laying offerings at Your feet, still there is no more joy for You to know than that our divine emperor (Domitian) returns from the northern climes.

Martial Epigrammata 10.28.1-2

Sower of the years, Janus, beginning of the shining and most beautiful world, with You begins our prayers and public vows.

Ovid Fasti 1.65-70

Biformed Janus, source of years gliding by in silence, who alone among the immortal celestials sees his own back, come, attend our nobles as Your guests, those whose labors secure delightful pastimes for the earth, and peace on earth, peace on the seas. Attend and bless Your Senators and those of the people of Rome, the Quirites, and with a nod open Your gleaming gates onto peaceful precincts.

Ovid Fasti 1.172

Janus, though I propitiate other Gods, I do offer wine and cakes to You first, so that I may obtain access through You, Janus, to any of the other Gods I may call upon.

Ovid Fasti 1.287

Janus, make peace and the servants of peace eternal. Grant that the author of peace may not desert his work.

Plautus Cistellaria 520

Thus is it true, by Jupiter, by Juno, and by Janus.

Varro Lingua Latinae 7.26 In the Carmen Salii

Arise, O Consus, arise. All things, truly, I entrust to Patulcium the Opener. Now You are Janus the Gatekeeper, now Cerus the Good Creator, now Janus the God of Good Beginnings. Come, now most especially, You who are the better of these kings.

Varro Lingua Latinae 7.27 In the Carmen Salii

Dance before the Father of the Gods, give thanks to the God of Gods.

10 PRAYERS TO JUNO

Apuleius Metamorphoses 6.4

Then kneeling, Psyche embraced the altar of Juno and, wiping at her tears, once more prayed. "O spouse and sister of Mighty Jupiter, whether You are worshipped and adored in the public rites of the temples of Samos, or whether You are called upon singularly by women in their tearful moment of giving birth, Your glory is nourished. You dwell in ancient temples, whether at haughty Carthage, whose temples You frequently bless when they celebrate Your journey from heaven on the back of a lion, or whether in Your temple beside the riverbank of Inachus where You are celebrated as the wife of thundering Jupiter Tonans and as Queen of the Gods. Famous among the Argives whose walls You defend, You who all the east venerates as Life-giving Zygia, who all the west names Lucina, may You be an advocate for me against my utter downfall, Juno Sospita, and endure until the end in all my weary labors, exhausted as I am, deliver me from imminent peril and free me from my fears, for I know You are accustomed to come of Your own accord to the assistance of such women who are pregnant and in danger."

Corpus Inscriptiones Latinae VI 32323, Acta Sacrorum Saecularium, Rome, Lines l21-22; ref. 92-99

Juno Regina, as it is prescribed for you in those books – and for this reason may every good fortune attend the Roman people, the Quirites – let sacrifice be made to You with a fine cow. I beg and pray [that You may increase the sovereign power and majesty of the Roman people, the Quirites, in war and peace; as You have always watched over us among the Latins. Forever may You grant safety, victory and health to the Roman people, the Quirites. May You bestow Your favor on the Roman people, the Quirites, and on the legions of the Roman people, the Quirites. May You preserve the health and welfare of the people of Rome, the Quirites, and may You always remain willingly favorable and propitious to the people of Rome, the Quirites, to the college of the quindecimviri, to me, to my house and household. May You accept [this sacrifice of (a fine cow), to be burnt whole for You in sacrifice. For these reasons may You be honored and strengthened with the sacrifice of this female (cow), and become favorable and propitious to the Roman people, the Quirites, to the college of the quindecimviri, to myself, to my house, and to my household.]

Corpus Inscriptiones Latinae VI 32323, Acta Sacrorum Saecularium, Rome, 17 BCE Lines 125-31

Juno Regina, if there is any better fortune that may attend the Roman people, the Quirites, we one hundred and ten mistresses of households of the Roman people, the Quirites, married women on bended knee, pray that You bring it about, we beg and beseech that You increase the power and majesty of the Roman people, the Quirites in war and peace; and that the Latins may always be obedient; and that You may grant eternal safety, victory and health to the Roman people, the Quirites; and that You may protect the Roman people, the Quirites, and the legions of the Roman people, the Quirites; and that You may keep safe and make greater the state of the Roman people, the Quirites; and that You may be favorable and propitious to the Roman people, the Quirites, to the quindecimviri sacris faciundis, to us, to our houses, to our households. These are the things that we one hundred and ten mistresses of households of the Roman people, the Quirites, married women on bended knee, pray, beg, and beseech.

Corpus Inscriptiones Latinae VI 32329. 10 sqq. Acta Sacrorum Saecularium addition

Juno Regina, we, one hundred and ten the mothers of the families of the people of Rome, the Quirites, pray You allow what is now beneficial to the people of Rome, the Quirites, may then be made better, and we brides implore You to aid and increase the sovereign power and majesty of the people of Rome, the Quirites, in war and peace, and always to watch over the fame of the Latins. And may You favor the people of Rome, the Quirites, and the legions of the people of Rome, the Quirites, and preserve the republic of the people of Rome, the Quirites, and may You willingly favor and prosper us, our homes, and our families. This is what the one hundred and ten mothers of the families of the people of Rome, the Quirites, we brides of our families, pray, entreat, and implore (You to grant.)

Livius Andronicus Equos Troianos

Grant me the strength, Goddess, to whom I ask, to whom I pray; extend your assistance to me.

Da mihi hasce opes, quas peto, quas precor porrige opitula

Plautus Amphitryon 831-834

By the Highest Gods ruling in the heavens, by Juno, too, She whom most of all I fear and venerate, I swear that no mortal man has ever come near enough to touch me or in any way impugn upon my chastity or has give me cause for shame.

Seneca Hercules on Oeta 256-62

Wherever You may be in the ethereal regions, O wife of Jupiter Tonans, send a wild beast against Alcides as may satisfy my need. If a serpent moves through the marsh with a fruitful head, more vast than all others born in this region, if a feral beast lives that is so immense, so dire, so horrible that Hercules Himself would avert His eye, let this beast come forth from some vast cave.

Silius Italicus Punica 7.78-85

Be present O Queen of the Heavenly Gods, we Your chaste daughters pray and bring forth this venerable gift, we, all the Roman women of noble name, have woven this mantle with our own hands, embroidered it for You with threads of gold. This veil You shall wear for now, O Juno, until we mothers grow less fearful for our sons. But if You will grant that we may repel these African storm clouds from our land, we shall set upon You a flashing crown of diverse gems set in gold.

Statius Thebaid 10.67-69

Look, O Juno, upon the sacrilegious citadel of the Cadmean whore, and cast asunder that rebel mound. O Queen of Heaven, who rules the stars circling about the northern pole, with another thunderbolt, for You have the power, drive out Thebes as well.

Tibullus 4.6.1 ff.

Accept, O Juno Lucina, this offering of incense. Cheerfully, O Lucina, she has come to adorn your shrine of matrons...

Come, most chaste Queen of Heaven, appear in royal robes and nod your assent to the wine that is poured and the cakes piled high to await you. With you bring every herb for ending pain, and soothing songs to sing; across the ocean from distant shores bear such herbs as will cure our most severe ills, or whatever else we most fear. Rack this girl no more with pain, or cruelly delay her birthing.

Valerius Flaccus Argonautica 1.80-90

Almighty Queen of Heaven, remember when Jupiter made the skies grow wild with black clouds and sheets of rain; remember when Thundering Jupiter commanded Your return to the marriage bed and how You, frightened with sudden capture and at being left destitute following Your rape, sought only how to flee; remember how it was I who carried You upon my shoulders across the storm swollen Enipeus, when it carried away its banks to flood the Thessalian plane, and all were carried before its torrents. Grant, Juno, that I may arrive safely to Scythia where the Phasis flows. And You, virgin Minerva, snatch me away from harm. I, even I then, will set that plucked fleece in your shrine, and my father, relieved and grateful, will dedicate snow- white cattle from herds and lead them to Your altar with gilded horns.

Virgil Aeneid 6.195-98

Be my guide, if there is any way, and make Your course from the sky above into this grove, where rich boughs shade fertile land. And you, Holy Mother, do not desert us in our hour of indecision.

11 PRAYERS TO JUPITER

L. Accius Aenead sive Decius fr. 4

Invincible Holiness, with venerating prayers I ask that You send good portents to signify a change for the better for the people of our nation.

Cato Origines I fr. 12

The Latins vowed: Jupiter, if it is greatly pleasing to You, that we, rather than Mezentium, should give offerings to You, accordingly may You make us victorious.

Cato De Agricultura 132

Jupiter Dapalis, it is a tradition in my family that a cup of wine be offered to You in thanksgiving for the sacred feast. For this reason may You accept this feast offering. Jupiter Dapalis, may You be strengthened by this feast, may You be warmed by this small portion of our wine that I offer.

Cato De Agricultura 134

Jupiter, in offering You this fertum bread I pray good prayers in order that, pleased with this offering of fertum, You may be favorable to me and my children, to my house and our household. Jupiter, be strengthened by this fertum, be warmed by this small portion of our wine.

Catullus 64.171

Jupiter Almighty, if only in an earlier time Attic prows had never touched Cretan shores.

Catullus 66.30

How often Jupiter have You dabbed Your sorrowful eyes (at the death of a lover)?

Catullus 66.48

O Jupiter, may the whole race of Chalybes, the first to mine ore underground, the first to work raw metal into bars (and weapons), may they all be cursed.

Cicero De Domo sua ad Pontifices 144

O Jupiter Capitolinus, to You I pray, I entreat You, who the Roman people have named Optimus after Your kindness and Maximus after Your great power.

Cicero In Verrem Act. II Lib. V 184 sqq.

Now I pray to You, Jupiter Optimus Maximus, for You Syracusa raised this royal gift, worthy of Your most beautiful temple, worthy of the Capitolium and the Arx, that all nations deem a worthy service. Hands then raised to You in vows and promises turned to heinous wickedness to wrench the most holy images and most beautiful statues that Syracusa had erected in Your honor.

Corpus Inscriptiones Latinae III 1933 Public dedication, Salona, Dalmatia

Jupiter Optimus Maximus when today I will give and dedicate this altar to you, according to the laws, and within this region, whose laws and boundaries I will give and dedicate this very day, for as long as this palus stone shall remain beneath this altar. If anyone should sacrifice a victim and not have first thoroughly stretched out and examined the entrails, all the same may it be regarded as properly offered. Let the law of this altar be the same as those proclaimed for the altar of Diana on the Aventine Hill, what is said in those laws shall apply in this region as well. Thus for the reasons I have spoken, I give, I order, and I dedicate this altar to you, Jupiter Optimus Maximus, in order that you may be willing to be favorable and propitious to me, to my colleagues, to the colony's council of ten magistrates, to the people of the colony Martia Julia Salonia and to our wives and children.

Corpus Inscriptiones Latinae VI 2065 Fratres Arvales

O Jupiter Optimus Maximus, if You allow the emperor ...and [the Fratres Arvales] for whom I speak, to live uninjured and keep their homes safe, then come next 3 Jan., voted by the people of Rome, the Quirites, for the benefit of the Republic of the Roman people, the Quirites, [a sacrifice will be offered.] Should You preserve today's emperor and the people in good health from danger, if they remain as they are today as far as possible, and the results are beneficial as I have spoken, and, too, if You will grant to the emperor and this state as they are now or You will preserve them in a better state, thereby making it so, then in the name of the College of the Fratres Arvales I vow to You to sacrifice two bulls with gilded horns in the future.

Jupiter Optimus Maximus, for the same reasons given earlier today when (2) bulls with gilded horns were vowed to You in the future, what this day was vowed with these very words, and if You will make it so, then I vow to You an [additional] gift worth 25 pounds of gold and 4 pounds of silver to be drawn from the wealth of the Fratres Arvales in whose name I speak

Corpus Inscriptiones Latinae VI 30975

By Mercury, Jupiter, the God Eternal, Juno Regina, Minerva, Sol, Luna, Apollo, Diana, Bona Fortuna, Ops, Isis, Pietas, and the divine Fates, may it be good, fortunate and happy.

Corpus Inscriptiones Latinae VI 32 323. Acta Sacrorum Saecularium

105-7; and 93-99

Jupiter Optimus Maximus, as it is prescribed for you in the Sibylline Oracles –and for this [reason] may good fortune attend the Roman people, the Quirites – let sacrifice be made to you with this fine bull. I beg you and pray. I beg you and pray that you may increase [the power and majesty of the Roman people], the Quirites, in war and peace; [and that the Latins may always be obedient; and that you may grant eternal safety], victory and health [to the Roman people, the Quirites; and that you may protect the Roman people, the Quirites, and the legions of the Roman people], the Quirites; [and that you may keep safe and make greater] the state of the Roman people, [the Quirites, and that you may be] favorable and propitious [to the Roman people], the Quirites, to the collegium of the quindecimviri, [to me, to my house, to my household; and that] you may accept [this] sacrifice of [bull], to be burnt whole for you in sacrifice. For these reasons be honored with the sacrifice of this [bull], become favourable and propitious to the Roman people, the Quirites, to the collegium of the quindecimviri, to myself, to my house, to my household.

Corpus Inscriptiones Latinae XIV 03557 Tibur, Latium

IOVI CUSTODI SACRUM M AEMILIUS FLACCUS Q(AESTOR)

Fratres Arvales

Jupiter Optimus Maximus, to You we pray, we plead, we entreat in order that the emperor Caesar Hadrian, son of Nerva Trajan Augustus Germanicus, our prince and patron (of our college), the

Pontifex Maximus, having the powers of the Tribune of the People, Father of the Fatherland, we feel to say he will be well and prosperous as he travels from this place and province, over whatever lands or seas, returning safely and victorious in whatever matters he now undertakes. Grant him good results, and to this state, as it is now, or as it may improve in the future, keep him safe, and allow him to return to us safely and victorious. Also, may You first stop in the city of Rome. And if You make it to be so, then we vow to You, in the name of the College of the Fratres Arvales, in the future (to sacrifice) oxen with gilded horns

Horace Satires II.3.283-4

Spare me alone, (Jove); it is but a little thing to ask. Spare me only from death. Truly, for the Gods it is something easily done.

Horace Satires II 3.288-92

For a child lying sick in bed for five long months, a mother calls out, O Jupiter, who gives and takes away great anguish, if the quartan ague leaves my child, then on the day You indicate to hold a fast, nude he shall stand in the Tiber River.

Horace Satires II.6.22-23

It is enough to pray, Jupiter, who gives and takes away; may You grant me life; may You grant me the means, and I shall provide a balanced mind myself.

Horace Epistles I 18.107-12

May I have what I have now, and also a little more, that, the Gods willing, I may yet live what remains of a lifetime. May I have enough books and provisions to last the year, and not wallow in doubts with hopes wavering each hour.

Horace Carmina 1.12.49-52

Jupiter, father and guardian of mankind, descended from Saturnus, to You is given the care of mighty Caesar's fate; may Your will reign supreme while Caesar rules.

Juvenal X 185

Grant me a great length of life, O Jupiter, give to me many years.

Livy 1.10.6

Jupiter Feretrius, I, Romulus, myself a king and victor, bring to You these arms taken from a king, and in this precinct, whose boundaries I have imagined in my mind and will with purpose trace, I dedicate a shrine to receive the spolia opima which posterity will place here in your honor, following my example, taken from the kings and generals of our foes slain in battle.'

Livy 1.12.4-7

O Jupiter, it was through Your omen that I was led while I laid here upon the Palatine Hill, to establish the very first foundations of the city of Rome. Already the Arx, that fortress wickedly bought, is seized by the Sabines, from whence they, with sword in hand, now advance across the valley against us. But if You, Father of the Gods and of men, hold back our enemies, at least from this spot, delivering the Romans from their terror, and stay their shameful retreat, then this I vow to You, Jupiter Stator, that a holy precinct and shrine will be built in Your honor as a memorial to remind our descendents of how once the city of Rome was saved by Your aid.

Livy 1.18.9

Father Jupiter, if it is heaven's will that this Numa Pompilius, on whose head I place my hand, should become king of Rome, then may You signify Your will to us with certain signs within the boundaries that I have designated.

Livy 1.24.7-9

Hear, o Jupiter; hear me, too, Pater Patratus of the people of Alba! Hear me also, people of Alba! As these provisions have been written in good faith and publicly read from beginning to end from these tablets, and inasmuch as they have today been most clearly understood, so the People of Rome will not be the first to withdraw from these treaty provisions. If, in their public council, they were to do so, with false and malicious intent break this treaty, then, Dispater, on that day, may You bring ruin on the People of Rome, even as today I shall strike this swine, and strike them so much more the greater, as Your power and might is greater.

Livy 1.32.9

Hear, o Jupiter, and You Janus Quirinus, and all You heavenly Gods, and You gods of earth and of the lower world, hear me! I call You to witness that this people'-- mentioning it by name-- 'is unjust and does not fulfill its sacred obligations. But about these matters we must consult the elders in our own land in what way we may obtain our rights.

Livy 6.16.1

Jupiter Optimus Maximus, Juno Regina, Minerva, and all you other gods and goddesses who dwell upon the Capitolium and the Arx, is this how you allow your defender, the protector of your shrines, to be treated, to be vexed and harassed by his enemies in this manner? Shall this right arm which drove the Gauls headlong from your shrines now be bound and chained?

Livy 8.5

Listen, O Jupiter, to this wickedness. Listen, too, Justice and Lawfulness!

Livy 8.6.5

There is a heavenly power and You do exist, O great Jupiter; not in vain did we consecrate this seat to You, Father of Gods and Mankind.

Livy 8.9.6-8

Janus, Jupiter, Father Mars, Quirinus, Bellona, Lares, You divine Novensiles and You divine Indigetes, deities whose power extends over us and over our foes, and to You, too, Divine Manes, I pray, I do You reverence, I crave Your grace and favor will bless the Roman People, the Quirites, with power and victory, and will visit fear, dread and death on the enemies of the Roman People, the Quirites. In like manner as I have uttered this prayer so do I now on behalf of the commonwealth of the Quirites, on behalf of the army, the legions, the auxiliaries of the Roman People, the Quirites, devote the legions and auxiliaries of the enemy, together with myself to Tellus and the Divine Manes.

Livy 22.53.10-12

I swear with a deep conviction of mind that I shall never allow myself to desert the Republic of the people of Rome. If I should willfully break my oath, may Jupiter Optimus Maximus inflict upon me the worst, most shameful ruin, and on my house, my family, and all I possess.

Martial Epigrammata VII 60

Jupiter, sacred ruler on Tarpeian Heights, who we call Thunderer, let other men petition You and request Your divine favor, while Caesar is safe. But be not wroth with me if nothing I desire, and nothing for my own bounty I ask, and all my prayers to the heavens are made for Caesar's good health, for all I truly need, from Caesar it is freely given.

Ovid Fasti III 365-6

The time has come, Jupiter, to fulfill Your promise made in good faith.

Ovid Fasti IV 827-32

Then king Romulus said, As I found this city, be present, Jupiter, Father Mars, and Mother Vesta, and all gods who it is pious to summon, join together to attend. Grant that my work may rise with Your auspices. Grant that it may for many years hold dominion on earth, and assert its power over the east and west.

Ovid Fasti 4.893

To the Tyrrhenian king is vowed the enemy's vintage; You, Jupiter, will carry the unwatered wine from the cultivated vines of Latium.

Ovid Fasti 5.716-18

Then Pollux said, "Gather in my words, Father, and grant that the heavenly abode You reserved for me alone may be shared, for then half of the whole shall be a greater gift.

Ovid Heroides XIII 49-50

O Gods, I pray, spare us from sinister omens, and grant that my good husband shall return home from the wars to hang his arms before Jupiter Redux

Ovid Metamorphoses VII.615-21

Jupiter, if what they say is not false, if You did indeed embrace my mother Aegina, if then, great Father, You are not ashamed to acknowledge me as Your son, either restore to me what is mine or else build me a sepulcher as well." Then Jupiter sent lightning and thunder as a sign that He had heard. "I accept this to be Your sign and I pray that it is a good omen of Your approval.

Persius Satura III 35-38

O Mighty Father of the Gods, may it be your will to punish those cruel tyrants who are moved by an impetuous character steeped in dread desires, that they may look upon Virtue and melt away because they have abandoned Her.

Persius Satura X. 185

Grant me long life, O Jupiter, give me many years.

Petronius Satyricon 98

In You, dearest Father, in Your hands do we place our safekeeping.

Petronius Satyricon 122.156-8

Jupiter Almighty and Tellus, daughter of Saturnus, I, who willingly have borne arms in Your defense and who in the past has honored You with my triumphs, I swear, that it is by Your will that I am now invited to raise my hand in anger, and not by my will that Mars the God of War now inspires this army with His avenging fury.

Petronius Satyricon 126

What has happened, Jove, to make You throw down Your arms, to become an old story in heaven, to disdain these terrestrial charms? Here now was a worthy occasion to beetle your brows and put on the horns of a bull, or else to don the feathers and beak of a swan. Here is a real Danae, she would kindle Your lust even higher. One touch, one mere touch of her body would melt Your limbs in the fires of desire.

Plautus Menaechmi 617

By Jove and all the gods I swear.

Per Iovem deosque omnis adiuro.

Plautus Cistellaria 520

It is true, by Jupiter, by Juno and by Janus.

Enim vero me Iuppiter, itaque me Iuno, itaque Ianus ita.

Plautus Trinummus 447

It is so, may Jupiter love me.

Ita, me amabit Iuppiter.

Plautus Pseudolus 13

May Jupiter prevent it [from happening] to you!

Id te Iuppiter prohibessit!

Plautus Aulularia 776

May Great Jupiter do with me as he wills.

Tum me faciat quod volt magnus Iuppiter!

Plautus Poenulus 1187-89

O Iuppiter, who does cherish and nurture the human race, through whom we live and draw the breath of being, in whom rest the hopes and lives of all humankind, I pray You grant that this day may prosper that which I have in hand.

Plautus Captivi 922; 976-7)

To Jove and the Gods I deservedly give great thanks...Jove Supreme, look down and keep me and my son, I do beseech you by your good genius. Come out! I want you.

Plautus Amphitryon 933-4

If in that I should fail, then, mighty Jupiter, I pray that you will forever let your anger fall on (me).

Plautus Persa 251-6

O Jove, opulent, glorious son of Ops, deity supreme, powerful and mighty, bestower of wealth, good hopes and bounty, gladly I give you thanks and duly offer praise also that all the gods kindly bestow this generous benefit by enabling me to help my friend in his need with an opulent loan.

Plautus Captivi 768-775

Great Jupiter supreme, you who are my patron god, it is you who makes me rich and givest to me wealth in sumptuous abundance, honor and gains, and games and play and festivals, and trains of servants bringing meat and drink, fullness and joy! It is certain now that I do not need to beg of any man. Nay, for now I can do a good turn for a friend, or ruin a foe. The pleasure of my days is brought to such sweet delight, with an ample heritage to pass on with all attachments worn away .

Plautus Persa 753-6

Now our foes are beaten and our citizens safe, our state at peace, peace assured, and the war brought to a triumphant conclusion, with our army and garrisons intact, I thank you, Iuppiter, for your kindly aid, and all the other divine powers of heaven, that I am avenged on my enemy.

Plautus Amphitruo 1022)

May Jupiter and the gods be angry with you, so that you live in eternal misery.

Plautus Captivi 909-910

May Jupiter and the Gods destroy you, and your stomach, and all the parasites that dwell in it, and all those who shall encourage them henceforth

Plautus Curculio 26-7

No, of course not, may Jupiter forbid it.

Nemini, nec me ille sirit Jupiter.

Plautus Pseudolus 13

May Jupiter prevent it (from happening to you).

Id te Juppiter prohibessit.

Propertius 2.28a. 1-2

O Jupiter, may You finally show compassion for this ill-stricken girl, the death of one so beautiful would cause Your reproach.

Propertius 4.10.15

Jupiter, today let these offerings fall in sacrifice to You.

Propertius 4.11.18

Grant, Father, what I have asked for my gentle shade.

Seneca Hercules Furens 205

Almighty Ruler from Olympus on high, Judge of All the World, set now a limit to my cares that have been for too long, and put an end to my disasters.

Seneca Hercules Furens 299

Ruler of the Gods, a hundred white bulls shall bleed for you. For you, Goddess of the Fruits of the Earth, your secret rites I will fund; in your shrine at Eleusius shall burn the sacred flame in celebration of your mysteries.

Seneca Hercules Furens 516

God of Gods, Ruler of the Heavens, who make men tremble in fear at your hurling lightning bolts, look now upon the hand of this dread king.

Servius Honoratus Ad Aeneis 3.89

Grant, Father, an augury.

Silius Italicus Punica 3.565-7

Give us an abode, Father, where at last the ashes and sacred relics of fallen Troy may rest, and where the rites of the royal Lares and the mysteries of Vesta may be safely kept.

Silius Italicus Punica 4.126-127

I recognize You, Mightiest of the Gods; Be present now, Father, and confirm the omen of Your eagle.

Silius Italicus Punica 6.466-72

Then (Regulus) lifted hand and eye together to the heavens, "O Giver of Justice and Rectitude, You who steers the course of the lingering stars of destiny, and Fides, no less divine to me, and Juno of Tyre, You Gods I invoked to witness my oath that I would return. If now I am permitted to speak words that will befit me, and by my voice protect the hearths of Rome, willingly I will go to Carthage, keeping my promise to return and endure whatever punishment is prescribed.

Silius Italicus Punica 10.432-8

O Father Jupiter who inhabits the Tarpeian Heights as His chosen abode next to the heavens, and You Juno, Daughter of Saturnus, who has not yet changed from Her hatred of the Trojans, and You, divine Virgin, whose gentle breast is harshly girt with the aegis of the terrible Gorgon, and all You Gods and Indigites of Italy, hear me as I swear by Your divine powers, and by the head of my father, who I hold no less to be a divine power, on my oath I swear.

Silius Italicus Punica 12.643-5

Grant, Mightiest of the Gods, that by Your hand, Father, the Libyan shall fall in battle to a thunderbolt, since by no other hand than Yours is there power to slay him.

Silius Italicus Punica 14.440-1

Bring forth, Father, Jupiter Ammon, bring your aid, Prophet of Garamantes, and grant a certain flight for my missile that it may impale an Italian .

Silius Italicus Punica 15.362-3

Grant, O Most Highest of the Gods, that I may preside over offering to You the choicest spoils, taken from the Libyan general (Hannibal), and borne on these my son's shoulders.

Statius Silvae I.1.74-78

Hail, Child of the Mighty, Father of the Gods, whose divine power I have heard from afar. In one moment my pool is blessed with happiness, at another it is venerated, made holy by Your presence, ever since I was granted to know that You are never far from me, and was enabled to watch Your immortal radiance from a vicinity near my abode.

Statius Thebaeid III.471-96).

Jupiter, God Almighty, You are, as we are so taught, He who imparts counsel to swift wings, and You who fills birds with foreknowledge of the future, and brings to light the omens and causes that lurk within the heavens, - not Cirrha can more surely vouchsafe the inspiration of her grotto, nor those Chaonian leaves that are famed to rustle at your bidding, Jupiter Dodona, in Molossian groves, though arid Hammon envy, and the Lycian oracle of Apollo contend in rivalry, and the Apis bull of the Nile, and Branhus, whose honor in Miletus is equal to his father Apollo's, and Pan, whom the rustic neighbors hear nightly along the wave beaten shores of Pisa, beneath Lycainian shades. More enriched in mind is he, for whom You, O Dictaean Jupiter, announce Your will in the favoring flights of birds. Wondrous the reason, but once, long ago, this honour was given to the birds, whether from His heavenly hall the Creator Himself granted it, sowing into fertile fabric of Chaos the hidden Nature of new things; or whether birds first took flight on the winds after evolving from forms that were originally like our own; or because their flight to learn the truth takes them nearer to the purer poles of the sky, from where wickedness is banished, and rarely do they alight on the earth; all this, Highest Father of the Gods and of the earth, is already known by You. May You allow that, guided by the skies, we shall have foreknowledge of the assembly of Argive forces and their initial movements in the fight ahead. If the Fates have resolved for the Lernaean spear to pierce the Echionian gates, then grant us signs and thunder on the left. Then let every bird in the heavens resound with his or her arcane language in confirmation. If, though, You prohibit this, then weave delays and on the right disguise the day's abyss with winged creatures.

Statius Thebaeid VI.197-201).

Faithless Jupiter, once I vowed these golden locks to You, accepting before I spoke that I would be bound by our pact, if at the same time You would grant me to offer my youthful son's manhood at Your temple. But far from that, Your priest would not confirm Your agreement to our pact, and instead my prayers condemned him. Then may his shade, who is worthier than You, receive them.

Tacitus Annales 16.35

We pour out a libation to Jupiter the Liberator. Observe, discover, and may the Gods avert the omen from you, my son, but you are born into a time when it is expedient to fortify your spirit with examples of courage and firmness of mind in the face of adversity.

Tacitus Histories IV 58

I implore and entreat you, Jupiter Optimus Maximus, to whom for eight hundred and twenty years we have paid the highest honors in so many triumphs, and I pray and venerate You Quirinus, Father of the City of Rome, if You would not be pleased to see this camp remain pure, preserved and inviolate under my command, may You at least not allow it to be polluted and defiled by a Tutor and a Calssicus. Grant that the soldiers of Rome may either be innocent of a crime, or at least may they be granted a speedy repentance without punishment.

Tiberianus IV

God Almighty, potent in all things, to Whom the aged Pole Star looks upon with admiring wonder, revering Your agelessness, the One who is always known by a thousand virtues, no one shall ever be able to account their countless number or timelessness. Now be addressed, if by any name Your dignity may be addressed, Holy One, be delighted, Unknown One, for Whom mightiest Earth trembles and the wandering stars halt their rapid course. You alone, though within Yourself are You many, You are first, and You are last, and likewise are You in between, arising above and outliving the very stars. For without end Yourself, You bring ever-gliding time to an end. On high from eternity You look upon the whirling course of Nature's certain Fate and of lives taken into the intricate convolutions of time immemorial only to be brought back once more and restored to their heavenly vault, the world no doubt restored of those parts drawn off and will have been lost, only once more for them to ebb back into the flow of unending time. If indeed it is allowed to thoughtlessly direct one's senses toward You and attempt to grasp Your holy splendor, whereby You surround the immense vastness of the stars and embrace the far-flung aether with Your likeness, perhaps Your image appears in the momentary flash of lightning with limbs of flowing flames, in that You are the Radiance, who enlightens all the world beneath You and presses onward the sunlight into our days. In You are the entire race of Gods. You are the invigorating cause of all things. You are all of Nature, the One God innumerable. You are the generating power in the totality of all sexual procreation. (You manifest in many way), born once here as a God, born once here as a world, this home of Gods and mankind, Lucent, majestic source of the starry field in youthful bloom. Instill me with Your favoring breath, I pray, grant to one willing to know, the manner in which You father the world. Grant, Father, that I may come to know the august causes by which You once wove all things together to form the physical world of matter, and what texture of light, congruent and dissimilar, You once wove into it, by which You animated the world with soul, and what it is that is lively, by which the quick body lives.

Tibullus 1.351-2

Spare me, Father Jove, I need not tremble for promises broken, no vows to the gods with impious words have I spoken.

Valerius Flaccus Argonautica 4.474-6)

I pray first to You, thunderous Jupiter Tonans, that now finally You may spare me in my old age and lift the manner in which Your anger has been set upon me.

Valerius Soranus FPL fr.4; August. Civ. Dei 7.9

Almighty Jupiter, who both engendered and fathered kings, things, and gods, God of Gods, who are both One and All

Almighty Jove, progenitor of kings, things, and Gods, And Mother of the Gods

MEDITATIONS ON THE ROMAN DEITIES

Velleius Paterculus II 131

Jupiter Capitolinus, Mars Gradivus called progenitor and aide of the Romans, Vesta, perpetual guardian of fire, and whatever divine powers in this greatness of Roman sovereignty, the largest empire on earth, exulted to the highest dignity, to You the public voice calls to witness and to pray: guard, preserve, and protect this state, this peace, this prince, and those who succeed to the Senate, by their long standing, determined worthy to consider the most grave matters among mortals.

Virgil Aeneid I.731-5

Jupiter, giver of the laws of hospitality, as it is said, may you wish this day to be pleasing and prosperous for Tyrians and Trojans alike, and that our children's children shall remember this day. Let Bacchus, giver of gladness, and good Juno, and you as well, O Tyrians, join with us in friendship at our celebration.

Virgil Aeneid II.689-91)

Jupiter Almighty, if any prayers bend You, look upon us. This only, and, if our piety deserves, then grant us Your assistance, Father, and confirm all these portents .

Virgil Aeneid IV.206-10)

Jupiter Almighty, to whom now the tattooed people of Maurusia, feasting on couches, pour libations of wine, a gift of Laenean Bacchus, offered in Your honour. Do you look upon this, Father? Or is it without any reason that we join in empty prayers and tremble in fear when You hurl lightning bolts and light the clouds in blinding fires?

Virgil Aeneid V.687-93

Jupiter Almighty, if You do not yet detest every Trojan to a man, if You still regard our pious acts of old, Father, grant that the flames will now avoid our fleet, and may You pull the diminished people of

Troy away from destruction. Or else, if I so deserve, then send forth Your thunderbolt from above and cast those who remain into death, and by Your power rightly bury them.

Virgil Aeneid IX.495).

O Great Father of the Gods, have pity and with your lightning bolt strike down this detested head to Tartarus, for there is no other way to break off the bonds of this cruel life.

Virgil Aeneid IX.625-9

Jupiter Almighty, give your approval to my audacious venture, and each year I shall carry solemn gifts with my own hand to your temple, and I shall place before your altar a snow white bullock with gilded horns of gold, carrying his head held high like his proud mother, seeking to strike with his horns, as his hooves churn the sand along the seashore.

Virgil Aeneid XII.197-211

By these same deities I, Aeneas, swear, by the Earth and the Sea, by the stars and Latona's twin children, and dual-faced Janus, and the powers of the gods below, and the harsh shrines of Father Dis. May the Great Father hear my vow, he that sanctions alliances with his thunderbolt. I touch the altars, and by the fires and by the divine powers who I have called to witness, I so swear, that never shall I breach this alliance or the peace of Italy, no matter what or how things happen, nothing shall divert my will (to keep my vow), not even if waves would cover the earth, plunging all into deluge, and the Heavens fell into deepest Tartarus. (By this vow I swear to be bound), even as this scepter, (the scepter that he now held up in his right hand), shall never bud new foliage, or branch out to lend shade, once it was cut deep in the forest, seized from its mother tree, its leaves and branches now encased in steel; once a tree, now an artifact turned by hand, decorated with bronze, and given to the Latin fathers to bear.

12 PRAYERS TO THE LARES, MANES ET PENATES

Corpus Inscriptiones Latinae VI 18817

Whole-heartedly I pray to you, most holy Manes, may you admit my dear husband among you, and, may you want to be most indulging in this, that in the hours of the night I may see him and also be advised by him on what to do, in order that I may be able to swiftly and sweetly come stand by his side. VI 18817

Arnobius Adversus Nationes III 43

Come, Dii Penates, come Apollo and Neptune and all You Gods, and by Your powers may You mercifully turn aside this ill disease that violently twists, scorches and burns our city with fever.

Cato De Agricultura 139

This prayer is probably to be understood as directed toward the *Lares Rurales* (Lares of the fields) or *custodes agri* (guardians of the fields), probably the most ancient form of Lar.

A ritual before clearing a grove or tilling land

Since the Romans believed that every piece of land had its own deities, or *genii*, and that each tree had its own guardian spirit which dwelt within it, it was not considered proper either to disturb land or to cut down trees without sacrificing first to the gods who lived within them.

Cato gives two versions of this ritual; one to be performed when pruning a grove, and one when digging land. The two rituals are exactly the same, except that Cato suggests adding the words "for the cause of carrying out the work" when digging the land. These words seem grammatically designed to replace the words "for the pruning of this sacred place" in the original prayer, and Cato probably intended a substitution of one phrase for the other, according to which was most suitable, rather than a simple addition of extra words onto the end of the prayer. This ritual could be used in a modern garden, before carrying out jobs such as pruning, mowing or planting.

Latin	English
Lucum conlucare Romano more sic oportet.	It is proper to open out a grove in this way, according to the Roman manner.
Porco piaculo facito, sic verba concipito: "Si deus, si dea es, quoium illud sacrum est, uti tibi ius est porco piaculo facere illiusce sacri coercendi ergo harumque rerum ergo, sive ego sive quis issu meo fecerit, uti id recte factum siet, eius rei ergo te hoc porco piaculo inmolando	Offer for atonement a pig, recite words thus: "Be you god or be you goddess, to whom this place is sacred, as it is right to offer for atonement to you a pig for the pruning of this sacred place, on account of these and on account of these things, whether I or whether one ordered by me

bonas preces precor, uti sies volens propitius mihi domo familaeque meae liberisque meis; harumce rerum ergo macte hoc porco piaculo inmolando esto."

offered it, in order that it may have been done rightly, for the sake of this thing I pray good prayers to you for the sacrificing of this pig for atonement, that you may be favourable and gracious to me, to my family and house, to my children; for the sake of these things be honoured by the sacrificing of the pig for atonement."

Si fodere voles, altero piaculo eodem modo facito, hoc amplius dicito: "operis faciundi causa."

If you wish to dig, offer in the same manner for another atonement, say this in addition: "for the cause of carrying out the work."

Dum opus, cotidie per partes facito.

During the work, offer every day over some area.

Si intermiseris aut feriae publicae aut familiares intercesserint, altero piaculo facito.

If you will break off, or public or family festivals will interfere, offer for another atonement.

Ennius Annales 1 fr. 141

And you Lares, care for our house that you established.

Lucan Pharsalia 9.990

Gods of the cremated dead, who dwell within the ruins of Troy, and Lares of my Aeneas who now reside in the temples of Lavinium and Alba, where among their altars the fires of Troy still shine, and You, Pallas, whose pledge of safety was given with the Palladium, upon which no man may look, sheltered deep within Her shrine, look upon me, the most renowned descendent of your family. Piously I place incense upon Your ancient altars and rightly invoke You. Grant me success and happiness in all that follows and I shall restore Your people. In thanks shall the Italians restore Your Phrygian walls and a new Roman Troy arise!

Ovid Fasti 5.435-7

After he has cleansed his hands with pure fountain water, he takes up the black beans in his mouth and turns, casting them back over his shoulder as he says, "This I send to you, Manes, with these beans I redeem me and mine." When nine times he has says this, then he says, "Manes of my forefathers, leave this place." He looks back, the rite of purification he thinks completed.

Plautus

Plautus: Mercator 834-35

Divine Penates of our ancestors, to you I commend the good fortune of my parents, and to you, Spiritual Father of our family, that you safeguard them well.

Plautus: Mercator 865

Lares of the roadside, I call upon you to kindly protect me.

Plautus: Poenulus 950-3

MEDITATIONS ON THE ROMAN DEITIES

To you gods and goddesses who cherish this city, reverently I pray that the reason for my coming here may have a happy outcome. May the Gods keep faith.

deos deasque veneror, qui hanc urbem colunt, ut quod de mea re huc veni rite venerim, measque hic ut gnatas et mei fratris filium reperire me siritis, di vostram fidem. [Plautus' "Poenulus" at The Latin Library]

Plautus: Trinummus 39-41:

I adorn our Lar with a garland, so that we and our house may have good fortune, happiness and prosperity.

Larem corona nostrum decorari volo. uxor, venerare ut nobis haec habitatio bona fausta felix fortunataque evenat

Seneca Octavia 245

Rise up, Father, come forth from the gloomy shades and aid your daughter who calls to you, or else cleave open the earth to its Stygian depths, and at last let me plunge into its refuge.

Silius Italicus Punica 6.113

I swear by the Manes, spirits of my ancestors, whom I fitly worship.

Sulpicia 4.5.9

Grant, O natal Genius, all my heart's desires, and expensive incense I shall burn upon your altar.

Tibullus 1.1.19-24

Lares, and you gods also, who earlier made our household fruitful and fortunate, may you guard and bless the little that remains today on our farm. Lares, accept what your kindred present to you. For you a lamb shall be offered when around your altar you'll hear rustic boys shouting, "Io! Give us fine harvests and fruitful vines!"

Tibullus 1.10.15-25

Lares, gods of my fathers, preserve me! While young and still nursing, you guided me when I played at your feet. Let none profane your antique images: rough-hewn wooden statues set upon altars of upturned sod then dwelled among our grandfathers. In those days humble reverence provided you with sweet honey alone, you stayed in meager shrines made of twigs, in tattered robes the gods were pleased with offerings of grapes and wreathes of wheat set upon carved heads. Granted his wish, a man would bring you honey cakes and set his virgin daughters to attend your little shrines. Lares, turn away from us those who scheme against us with their bronze weapons.

Tibullus 2.2.1-9

Speak no ill words today, good men and women, as we honor our friend on his birthday. Burn frankincense, burn fragrant herbs from lands at the very ends of the earth, even those sent from Arabia. His own spirit comes to receive his honors, a holy wreath to crown his soft crown of hair. This pure nard distilled for his temples and, sated on wine and honey cakes, he gives his assent. And to you, Cornutus, may everything you wish for be granted.

Tibullus 3.4.1-2; 3-4; 95-6

O gods, may you bring better dreams than this evil vision that has awakened me from a peaceful sleep; let it not be a prophetic vision. Cast far away from me this vain and false vision, and cease plucking our intestines with your zealous inquiries. Gods, turn this cruel dream to good, as night into day, and bid the warm South wind to carry it away.

Valerius Flaccus Argonautica 3.448-55

Leave us, you ghosts of the slain, forget those angry memories and vengeful thoughts. Let peace come between us. May you grow to love your Stygian resting-place, far from our crew and far from the seas we travel, and may you stay far from the battles we engage. At no time haunt our cities back home in Greece or at the crossroads howl. Do no harm to our pigs and cattle, bring no pestilence to our herds or crops. Do not woefully assail our people or our children.

Valerius Flaccus Argonautica 4.674-75

Whosoever You may be among the Gods, I shall follow wherever You may lead, in faithful trust that You do not deceive.

Valerius Flaccus Argonautica 5.51-53

O Holy Ghost, I pray that you may come to us in the semblance of a guiding spirit with foreknowledge of impending storms and advising our helmsman on the course he must follow.

Valerius Flaccus Argonautica 5.192-209

Bearing sacramental wine in a heavy bowl he approaches the tomb and its altar and pours out the libation, addressing the ghosts of the dead. "Phrixus, hear me, your kinsman. I pray you be my guide in this enterprise. Protect us and help us now that we have reached this land, having survived the perils of the trackless seas we have crossed. Remember your countrymen in kindness, and favor your kinsfolk. And You, too, my Lady, at whose empty tomb I stand, a goddess now of the sea, be gracious to us and help us now and on our return when we venture again on your waves. When shall that golden fleece sail again past Sestus, perhaps to recognize that unfortunate stretch of water? And You, O woods and shores of Colchis, welcome us now and lead us to that sacred tree where the glittering fleece hangs. And you, O Phasis, child of potent Jove, accept and allow Minerva's vessel to travel between your banks on your tranquil current. Appropriate gifts I promise at shrines that I shall erect in your honour when I get home - statues commanding the reverence we pay to the Enipeus or the Inachus whose god lolls in his golden cave."

Valerius Flaccus Argonautica 6.288-91

Holy Father, give me the strength and courage to try to do you credit so that I may teach my children those lessons you once taught to me.

Virgil Georgics 1.498-501

Gods of our Fathers, Indigetes, heroes native to this land, Romulus and Mother Vesta, who preserve Etruscan Tiber and Roman Palatine, in this at least do not prohibit, a young savior come to the aid of a generation decimated by war.

Virgil Aeneid 2.701-4

Any moment now, without delay, I follow, and wherever You lead, there shall I be. Gods of my fathers, preserve my house, save my grandchildren. Yours this augury, and yours the holy powers in Troy.

Virgil Aeneid 4.576-79

We follow you, Holy One of the Gods, whoever you may be, and once again joyfully obey your command. Come, O Gentle One, and with favoring stars in the heavens, lend us your aid.

13 PRAYERS TO MAGNA DEUM MATER IDAE

Gaius Valerius Catullus 63.91:

O Goddess, Great Goddess Cybele, keep far away from me Divine Mistress of Dindymus, and all Your furies, too, (who cause men to castrate themselves in Your worship); may they all fall far away from my house. Go, incite others if You must, just go, and stay far away from me and my house.

IDR-03-05-01, 253, Alba Iulia Apulum, Dacia

Pro salute Augusti Magnae deum Matri sacrum Titus Flavius Longinus veteranus ex decurione alae II Pannoniorum decurio coloniae Dacicae decurio municipii Napocensis decurio Kanabarum legionis XIII Geminae et Claudia Candida coniunx et Flavius Longinus Clementina Marcellina filii ex imperio pecunia sua fecerunt locus datus decreto decurionum

"For health and wellbeing, Titus Flavius Longinus, veteran officer of the Second Pannonia Cavalry, senator of colony Dacia, decurion of Napocensis, cavalry officer of the Canabarian Thirteenth Legion Gemina, and his wife Claudia Candida and his children Flavius Longinus and Clementina Marcellina, under his own authority and at his own expense, by a decree of the city council, set up a sanctuary for the Augustan Great Mother of the Gods."

Julian the Blessed IV.112

Who is the Mother of the Gods? She is the source of the intellectual and creative gods, who, in their turn guide the visible gods: She is both the Mother and Spouse of mighty Jupiter; She came into being next to and together with the great creator; She is in control of every form of life, and the cause of all generation; She easily brings to perfection all things that are made, without pain She brings to birth, and with the Father's aid creates all things that are; She is the motherless maiden, enthroned at the side of Jupiter, and in very truth is the Mother of All the Gods. For having received into Herself the causes of all the gods, both intelligible and supramundane, She became the source of the intellectual gods.

Publius Ovidius Naso, Fasti 4.319-24

Nurturing Mother, fecund womb that bore the Gods, accept the prayers of this supplicant under one condition. I am said to be unchaste. If You condemn me, my confession I'll make and accept death as penalty for the verdict of a goddess. But if the crime is absent, pledge Your security for my life, grant this one thing in Your action, and follow chaste goddess my chaste hands.

RIB 1791 = CLE 24, Magnae (Caervoran), Britannia

Imminet Leoni Virgo caelesti situ spicifera iusti inventrix urbium conditrix ex quis muneribus nosse contigit deos ergo eadem mater divum Pax Virtus Ceres Dea Syria lance vitam et iura pensitans in caelo visum Syria sidus edidit Libyae colendum inde cuncti didicimus ita intellexit numine inductus tuo Marcus Caecilius Donatianus militans tribunus in praefecto dono principis

Tiberius Catius Asconius Silius Italicus, Punica 17.27-9:

(P. Scipio Nasica welcomes the Magna Mater at Her arrival to Rome) "after Her long voyage, with his hands held up in prayer."

But when the ship became stuck in the Tiber a priest called out: "Spare your guilty palms from touching these ropes. Away from here, I warn you, go far away from hence, whosoever among you is unchaste, do not share in this sacred task."

Tiberius Catius Asconius Silius Italicus, Punica 17.35-40: (Then Claudia took up the ropes alone)

O Great Mother of the Heavenly Host, Genetrix of all the divine powers, whose children cast lots to see who should rule over land, and seas, and the stars, and the nether world of the Manes, if without violation my body is free of all unchaste crimes, may You be my witness, dear Goddess, and testify on my behalf of my innocence by the ease with which I now draw this vessel.

Statius Thebiad 8.303-38

O eternal Creatrix of Gods and men, who animates forest and stream with soul, and joins seeds of life together throughout the world, and You bear the stones of Pyrrha that were enlivened into men by the hand of Prometheus. Hungry men You were first to give nourishment with a variety of foods. You encircle and carry the sea within You. Under Your power are the gentleness of domesticated herds and the ferocity of wild beasts and the repose from flight of birds. Firm and immobile, unsetting power of the earth suspended in the vacuum of space, You are the center around which the rapid heavens revolve. All the heavenly bodies, in chariots of fire, wheel about You, O center of the universe, indivisible from the Great Brotherhood of the Gods. Therefore are You the Bountiful who nourishes so many nations, and at the same time so many high cities and so many noble peoples. You provide Yourself and all the world as one, from above and below. You carry without effort to Yourself Atlas, who toils to hold up the celestial field of stars. We alone do You refuse to carry. Do we weigh You down, Goddess? For what unwitting wrong, I pray, must we atone? That we would so soon come here as a small band of strangers from distant Inachian shores? It is unworthy of You, most beneficial Goddess, to set limits by such cruel means on every side against all that is human merely by birth, against people who everywhere are Your own. May You then abide with and bear arms for all alike. I pray You allow that those warriors who spend their last breathe in the battle will have their souls return once more into the heavens. Do not so suddenly carry us off to our tomb and take the breath from our body. Do not be in such haste; soon enough we will come as all do when You lead them along the path that all must travel. Only listen to our pleas and keep a level plain for the Pelasgians and do not hasten the swift Fates. And You, dear to the Gods, not by any hand or Sidonian sword were you dispatched, but mighty Nature opened Her heart to you, entombing you for your merits in Cirrha's chasm, welcoming you in Her loving embrace. May You joyously grant, I pray, that I may come to know You in my prayers, that You may council me on the heavens and give true warnings from Your prophetic altars, and that You may teach me what You are prepared to reveal to people. I will perform Your rites of divination, and in Apollo's absence I will call Your prophet and upon Your divine spirit for visions. That distant place to which You hurry is, to me, more potent than all the shrines of Delos and Cirrha, better by far than the sanctuary of any other shrine.

Publius Vergilius Maro, Aeneid 10.252-5

Nurturing Idean Mother of the Gods, for whom Dindymus is dear, you who love turreted cities and bridled lions, lead me now into battle, and rightly fulfill the omens. Come with your favoring step, O Goddess, lead and we Phrygians will follow.

14 PRAYERS TO MARS

M. Porcius Cato De Agricultura 141

"Father Mars, I pray and beseech You, to be willing and propitious to me, to our household and to our family, for which I have ordered this suovitaurilia to be driven around my grain fields, my land, and my estate, in order that You may prevent, repel, and avert, seen and unseen <decay and> disease, deprivation, desolation, calamities, and intemperate weather; I pray You allow the fruits, the grain, the vines, and the bushes, to grow strong and well and be brought to the storage pit. May You also keep the shepherds and their flocks safe, and give good health and vigor to me, to the household, and to our family. To this end it is, as I have said - namely, for the purification and lustration of my estate, my land, and my grain fields, cultivated and uncultivated - that I pray You may be honored and strengthened by this suovitaurilia, these suckling sacrificial victims. O Father Mars, to this same end I pray that You bless these sucklings in sacrifice."

Claudius Claudianus In Rufinum 1.334-48

"Mars, whether you rush down from the cloud-capped Mount Haemus, whether on the frosty white mountains of Thrace, whether stirring on Monte Santo in Macedonia with the black boots of soldiers stationed on all the lands they hold, to make ready with me, and defend your Thrace, if it is made happy, the campaign coming into glory, the sacred oak will be dressed with an offering of spolia."

Hearing his prayer, Father Mars arose from the snow-topped crag of Mount Haemus exhorting His swift ministers: "Bellona, bring my helmet; attend me, Pavor, fasten the wheels upon my war chariot; Formido, bridle my swift horses in harness. Hastily press forward on your work. See, (he) makes ready himself for war; Stilicho whose habit it is to load me with rich trophies and hang upon the oak the plumed helmets of his enemies. For us together the trumpets ever sound the call to battle; yoking my chariot I follow wheresoever he pitches his camp."

Corpus Inscriptiones Latinae VI 2104, Rome, Carmen Fratrum Arvalium

Lasas assist us, Lasas delight us, Lasas come to our aid! Neither plague nor ruin, Marmor, allow to be visited on us. But if however we are invaded, like Mars we shall leap across our borders To sate you with the blood of our enemies and stay the barbarians. Marmor assist us, Marmor defend us, Marmor come to our aid. Triumph, triumph, triumph, triumph, triumph!

Gellius Noctes Atticae 13.23.13

When Titus Tatius spoke in favor of peace, among his words was this prayer, Neria, wife of Mars, I appeal to you, give peace. May you use your own favored position with your husband; counsel Him to partake in this plan. In the same way as we reconcile ourselves to those who carried off our daughters, may you now join with Him for all times in favoring His.

Horace Carmina 1.2.35-40

Father Mars, too long have You neglected to look upon Your nation and upon Your grandchildren. Alas, for too long have You been absent in the game of war. Recall Your delight in the clash of battle;

come, Mars, take pride once more in the sight of polished Roman helmets gleaming, and how the battle hardened legions meet the grimacing Maurians in battle. Come now, we pray.

Livy 8.9.6-8

Janus, Jupiter, Father Mars, Quirinus, Bellona, Lares, You divine Novensiles and You divine Indigetes, deities whose power extends over us and over our foes, and to You, too, Divine Manes, I pray, I do You reverence, I crave Your grace and favour will bless the Roman People, the Quirites, with power and victory, and will visit fear, dread and death on the enemies of the Roman People, the Quirites. In like manner as I have uttered this prayer so do I now on behalf of the commonwealth of the Quirites, on behalf of the army, the legions, the auxiliaries of the Roman People, the Quirites, devote the legions and auxiliaries of the enemy, together with myself to Tellus and the Divine Manes.

Livy 10.19.17-18

If today, Bellona, You grant us victory, a new temple I vow.

Livy 19.27.1 ff.

When dawn arrived Scipio emerged from his headquarters in ritual decorum to pray before the advance guard. He prayed, Gods and Goddesses who inhabit the land and sea, to You I pray and ask that whatsoever has been done under my auspices and my command, is now being done or shall be done, may prove beneficial for me, for the people of Rome and their children, and for our allies and the Latins, who joined with the Roman army under my auspices in waging war on land and sea. May Your good counsel and assistance be with me and may You bless all our endeavors with rich increase. May You guard the welfare and sustenance of our soldiers, allow the victors to return home healthy and safe, and laden with the spoils of victory. May they bring back honors and plunder to share in my triumphal procession after defeating our enemy. Grant to me and to the Roman people the power of vengeance and the opportunity and means to inflict on our enemies the same as the

Carthaginians have striven to inflict against the people of Rome and thereby an example shall be set for others.

Lucan De Bello Civili: Pharsalia 2.47-49

Gods above, we do not pray for peace. Grant rage onto the nations. May You now arouse the cities; bring forth the whole world in arms to war.

Macrobius Saturnalia 3.9.7-8: Scipio Africanus' evocation of the Gods of Carthage.

Whether you are a god or a goddess of these people who defends this city of Carthage, and you Most High, take back your favor in defense of this city and these people whom I attack. I pray, I beseech, I ask your indulgence, that you withdraw and desert these people and this city of Carthage, and that you relinquish the temples and sacred precincts of this city, go away without them, and incite these people and their city into fear of oblivion. Come then to favor Rome by crossing over to me and my army, and with our city tried and accepted as the location for your sacred precincts and holy rites, be propitious to me and the people of Rome, and my soldiers. If you make this happen, with clear and recognizable signs, I vow to erect temples for you and to initiate games in your honor.

Macrobius Saturnalia 3.9.10-11: The devotio of Carthage to the Gods of the Underworld

Dis Pater, Veiovis, and Di Manes, or with any other name by which it is proper to call You, since all in this city of Carthage and its army, who, I feel, fled before me in terror only because you filled them with alarm and fright, everyone who opposes our legions and the wall of shields of our army, and our missiles are carried forward on them by your hand, in this way you led away the enemy army and their soldiers. Their city and fields, and those who are in this place and this region, the lands and cities that they inhabit, you have now deprived them of the supreme light, their hostile army, their city and their lands. I feel to say that it was you who has devoted and consecrated this city and its lands, from the beginning and all time, that by law, who and when are made over and devoted as the highest sacrifices. Therefore, I who am victorious, by my faith as a magistrate of the people of Rome, and as commander of the armies, I give this vow on behalf of the people of Rome, our armies and legions, that you may retain everything born to this land and that grew in healthy by your aid. If you will make this happen, so that I may know, sense and derive that this has happened, then by whatever vow will have been made, wherever it will have been made, may it be properly made with sheep sacrificed upon the tribal altars. I call upon Tellus, Mother Earth, and You mighty Jupiter, to act as witnesses to my vow.

Ovid Fasti 3.1-2

Bellicose Mars, lay aside for awhile Your round bronze shield and spear. Mars, be present and let loose from its helmet Your sleek, shining hair.

Ovid Fasti 3.73-6

Arbiter of arms, from whose blood I am believed to have been born, and many the proofs I will give that are accepted, after You we will begin the Roman year, from Your name, Father, we will name the first month of the year.

Ovid Fasti 4.827

Then king Romulus said, As I found this city, be present, Jupiter, Father Mars, and Mother Vesta, and all gods who it is pious to summon, join together to attend. Grant that my work may rise with Your auspices. Grant that it may for many years hold dominion on earth, and assert its power over the east and west.

Ovid Fasti 5.573-77

If, Father, my war is authorized by Vesta's priestess, and whenever I prepare to take divine vengeance, Mars, be by my side and satiate cold steel with guilt's blood, and lend Your favour to the better side.

If I am victorious for You I'll build a shrine and call You Ultor, Mars the Avenger.

Plautus Bacchides 847-48

Mars and Bellona, never trust me again, if I do not make him breathless, if ever I should meet him once more and not take away his vital breath.

Silius Italicus Punica 3.126-27

But You, O (Mars) Father of Warfare, have pity on us, turn evil aside from us and preserve (my husband's) life as inviolable to all Trojan assaults.

Silius Italicus Punica 10.553-54

Father Mars, You who were not at all deaf to my vows, these men, survivors of the battle, dedicate to You the choicest armour of our victory trophies.

Valerius Flaccus Argonautica 5.250-52

Mars Gradivus, hear me, on whose sacred oak which fleece glitters. Protect it and keep it safe always, your arms prepared to clash at the clarion's sound to which your voice responds, ringing out in the darkness.

Vellius Paterculus II 131

Jupiter Capitolinus, Mars Gradivus called progenitor and aide of the Romans, Vesta, perpetual guardian of fire, and whatever divine powers in this greatness of Roman sovereignty, the largest empire on earth, exulted to the highest dignity, to You the public voice calls to witness and to pray: guard, preserve, and protect this state, this peace, this prince, and those who succeed to the Senate, by their long standing, determined worthy to consider the most grave matters among mortals.

Virgil Aeneid 12.176-82; 197-211

May the Sun now bear witness, and so too the Earth, I pray, for whom I have been able to endure these many labors, and you, Almighty Father, and you his consort, (Juno), daughter of Saturnus, at one time more beneficial, at another kinder, be so now as I pray to you, O Goddess, and to you, too, Father Mavors, who wields all warfare under your powers, and on all the springs and rivers of this land I invoke as witnesses, and all the powers of the high heavens and those of the deep blue seas on whom it is proper to call.

By these same deities I, Aeneas, swear, by the Earth and the Sea, by the stars and Latona's twin children, and dual-faced Janus, and the powers of the gods below, and the harsh shrines of Father Dis. May the Great Father hear my vow, he that sanctions alliances with his thunderbolt. I touch the altars, and by the fires and by the divine powers who I have called to witness, I so swear, that never shall I breach this alliance or the peace of Italy, no matter what or how things happen, nothing shall divert my will (to keep my vow), not even if waves would cover the earth, plunging all into deluge, and the Heavens fell into deepest Tartarus. (By this vow I swear to be bound), even as this scepter, (the scepter that he now held up in his right hand), shall never bud new foliage, or branch out to lend shade, once it was cut deep in the forest, seized from its mother tree, its leaves and branches now encased in steel; once a tree, now an artifact turned by hand, decorated with bronze, and given to the Latin fathers to bear.

15 PRAYERS TO MERCURIUS

Horace Satires 2.6.4-5

It is well. Nothing more ample do I pray, O Maia's son, save that You will make these my gifts last throughout my life.

Horace Satires 2.6.14-5

May You, Mercurius, make plump the riches of my house and all else there, spare my natural talents in any case, and as usual, may You remain the primary guardian over me.

Horace Carmina 1.10.1-8; 20-24

Mercurius, by Atlas born to Maia, God who fashioned our uncivilized ancestors into cultured men of urbane speech and athletic bearing, to You I sing, Messenger of the Gods and of mighty Jove, inventor of the curved lyre, it pleases You to compose secret jokes and play pranks skillfully. Gladly You restore pious souls to their proper places and by the golden staff confine the trivial quarrel. Dear are You to the Gods above and below.

Horace Carmina 3.11.1-8

Mercurius, once You taught Amphion how to move dumb stones by the power of song, and it was You who taught the tortoise shell to resonate with seven well placed strings, once silent and now beloved at monthly banquets and in temples, teach me now how to unstop Lyde's obstinate ears.

Manilius Astronomicon 1.30ff

Mercurius Cyllenius, principle author of all sacred knowledge, at times within Heaven, at other times travelling within the starry signs to open the celestial paths to the highest parts above and the lowest paths beneath the earth. You stitch together the stars in the empty void of space into constellations, name them and determine their course; may it have been for us to reverently use the greater powers of the universe that You make, pondering them, not in all matters, but in the potential of things in themselves, and to learn of the divine plan set for the greatest nations.

Martial Epigrammata 7.74

Mercury, Cyllene's Glory, Heaven's pride, Messenger with the clever tongue, around whose golden staff the serpent coil, may it shine brightly among the Gods. May You enjoy Your stolen loves, whether You desire Venus or Ganymede, and on the Ides may Your Mother's altar be adorned with laurels, and Your grandfather Atlas bear a lighter load, if You will allow Norbana and Carpus, who met for the first time today, to always celebrate their nuptials together. This a pious master of the arts offer a gift to Your wisdom, this incense I send to You, faithfully I pray, and faithfully also to Jupiter.

Ovid Fasti 5.447-8

Advise me, Pleiad Maia's son, Mercurius, god of the venerated potent staff, often have You seen the court of Stygian Jove.

Ovid Fasti 5.663-70

Glorious Mercury, grandson of Atlas, be present here today as You were once upon Arcadia's hill, a Pleiad's son by Jove. Arbiter in peace and in arms among the Gods of the heavens above and on earth, traveler on winged feet, You who enjoys the lyre and who takes pleasure in whoever glistens with the wrestler's ointment, You who has taught eloquent speech in all tongues, for You on the Ides of May, the Fathers once dedicated a sacred shrine near the Circus and named this day ever after to be Your feast day.

Ovid Fasti 5.681-90

(O Mercury) whether I have falsely called You to bear witness in the past, or deceitfully called upon Jupiter not to hear my empty promises, or if there is some other god or goddess that I knowingly deceived, wash away my past perjuries, wash away yesterday's perfidious words, and allow me new perjuries to make when the new day dawns, and make the gods be indifferent to my lies. Grant that I may profit, grant joy in making a profit, grant that I may enjoy once more swindling my customers with deceitful words.

Persius Satires 2.45

Lusting for wealth you slay an ox and call to Mercurius, "Grant that my Penates may fortunately prosper. Grant that my flocks and herds may be fertile."

Plautus Asinaria 545-6

Praise and thanks we ought justly to give to the great god of treachery (Mercurius), for surely there is no end in sight to our own slanderous ways, our deceitfulness or our slyness.

Plautus Stichus 402-5

Thanks be to Neptunus and the Tempestates, for returning me safely home again, my venture a success! And also to Mercurius, who helped me in my mercantile affairs and quadrupled my fortune with profit.

16 PRAYERS TO MINERVA

Cicero De Domo sua ad Pontifices 144

O Minerva, You have always come to my aid with Your counsels, witness to the existence of my works;

Corpus Inscriptiones Latinae VI 2065

Minerva, for what I have vowed today, in the same words that made my pledge to offer Jupiter Optimus Maximus an ox with gilt horns, [(being that) if You will grant Emperor Caesar Domitianus Augustus Germanicus, son of the divine Vespasian, pontifex maximus, having powers of the tribune of the people, censor in perpetuity, father of his country, and Dimitia Augusta, his wife, and Julia Augusta, for those whom I have named and also for all those others whom I have not named who live in their households on the third day before the Nones of January, and after them the people of Rome, the Quirites, and also for the Republic of the people of Rome, the Quirites, and if from this day You will preserve their health from peril, whereby they remain as they are today, or indeed their lot is improved by good results,] then if You would also make it so, then to You, in the same words, in the name of the college of Fratres Arvales I vow to sacrifice to You in the future an ox cow with gilt horns.

Corpus Inscriptiones Latinae XI 1305 Travi, Aemilia

To Minerva, in memory for restoring her hair, Tullia Superiana willingly and deservedly fulfills her vow.

CIL 11, 1306 = ILS 3137, Travi, Aemilia

Minervae / Medicae / Cardabiac(ensis) / Valeria / Sammonia / Vercellens(is) / v(otum) s(olvit) l(ibens) m(erito) AE 1962, 152, Visentium (Bisenzo), Etruria Minervae Nortinae sacr(um) L(ucius) Aebutius L(uci) f(ilius) Sab (atina) Saturninus

Livy 6.16.1

Jupiter Optimus Maximus, Juno Regina, Minerva, and all you other gods and goddesses who dwell upon the Capitolium and the Arx, is this how you allow your defender, the protector of your shrines, to be treated, to be vexed and harassed by his enemies in this manner? Shall this right arm which drove the Gauls headlong from your shrines now be bound and chained?

Ovid Fasti 6.652

Come now, golden haired Minerva, to favor the task I've begun.

Seneca Hercules Furens 900

To you, you alone, O warlike Pallas Minerva, I pray, friend and companion in all my toils; Tamer of Lycurgus, ivy wreathed you crossed the eastern seas, bearing the Thyrsus in your hand; and you divine twins, Apollo and Diana, hear my prayer.

Scriptores Historiae Augustae, Vita Probi c. 12.7

Jupiter Optimus Maximus, Juno Regina, and You virtuous dancer, Minerva, Concordia of the bereaved, Victoria of the Romans, grant this meeting of the Senate of the Roman people, grant these Roman soldiers, and those soldiers of our allies and of friendly foreign nations as well, that they will serve as he commands.

Statius Thebaid 2.715-42

Proud, warlike Goddess, great honor and wisdom of Your Father, powerful in war are You, on whom the grim helmet is borne with its frightful decoration, speckled with the Gorgon's blood that glows more violent with increasing rage, never has Mavors or Bellona with Her battle spear inspired more ardent calls to arms on the war trumpets than You. May You with Your nod accept this sacrificial offering. Whether You come from Mount Pandion to our rites by night, or from dancing happily in Ainian Itone, or from washing once more Your hair in the waters of Libyan Triton, or whether the winged axle of your war chariot, with its paired pure-bred horses carries you astride its beam, shouting aloud, now, to You, we dedicate the shattered spoils of virile men and their battered armour. Should I return to my Parthaonian fields, and upon being sighted Martian Pleuron should throw open wide her gates for me, then amid her hills, at the center of the city, I shall dedicate to you a golden temple where it may be your pleasure to look upon Ionian storms, and where Achelous tosses about his flaxen hair to disturb the sea where it leaves behind the breakers of Echinades. In here will I display accounts of ancestral wars and the death-masks of great hearted kings, and affix the arms of the proud in the rotunda that I have returned with myself, taken at the cost of my own blood, and those, Tritonia, that you will grant when Thebes is captured. There a hundred Calydonian virgins will serve in devotions at your altar, shall duly twine the Actaean torches, and weave from Your chaste olive tree purple sacrificial fillets with snow white strands of wool. At nightly vigils an aged priestess will tend your altar's fire, and never will she neglect to safeguard your modesty, attending in secret to the rites of your boudoir. To you in war, to you in peace, the first fruits of our labors shall be borne, without offence to Diana.

17 PRAYERS TO NEPTUNUS

Arnobius Adversus Nationes III 43

Come, Dii Penates, come Apollo and Neptune and all You Gods, and by Your powers may You mercifully turn aside this ill disease that violently twists, scorches and burns our city with fever.

Horace Carmina 1.5.6-16

(O Neptune) Soon he'll...stare in wondering shock At winds gone wild on blackening seas! ...how false the breeze can blow. Pity all those who have not yet found Your glossy sweetness churned! My shipwreck's tale Hangs, told in colours, on Neptune's temple wall, a votive Plaque, with salvaged clothes Still damp, vowed to the sea's rough lord.

Lucan Pharsalia 4.110-13

May it be your will, O supreme Father of the Universe, and Yours also, O Neptune, to Whom the lot fell second and gave an equal power of the trident over the seas. May You above impede the air with perpetual storm clouds; and You below forbid to turn back each surge of the sea You send forth.

Ovid Metamorphoses 8.595-602

O Neptune, who reigns over the realm of wandering waves, Bearer of the Trident, come to our aid, I pray, and undo her father's savagery. Neptune, grant her a safe haven, or else allow her to become a place herself, (to live forever as one of Your nymphs).

Petronius Arbiter Satyricon 108

O Gods, help us! Who takes up arms and beckons death amid the waves, or inadequate to suffer one death? The sea's savagery is enough, send no fresh floods to swell the savage waves.

Plautus Rodens 906-910:

Thanks be to Neptune my patron, who dwells in the fish-teeming salt sea, for speeding me homeward from his sacred abode, well laden and in a good hour.

Plautus Stichus 402-5

Thanks be to Neptunus and the Tempestates, for returning me safe home again, my venture a success! And also to Mercurius, who helped me in my mercantile affairs and quadrupled my fortune with profit.

Plautus Trinummus 819-30

O Neptunus, brother of Jove and Nereus, heartily and gladly I give you praise and grateful thanks. And to you, Neptunus, before all other gods I offer and accord you the highest thanks. I give you praise, for you know how to treat men fairly; this befits the Gods.

Sillius Italicus Punica 15.159-62

Neptune, divine Lord of the Trident, on whose high seas we begin to cross, if my preparations are made justly, grant our fleet to sail safely, Father, and do not scorn to aid our labors. The war I now draw across the sea is a just war.

MEDITATIONS ON THE ROMAN DEITIES

Statius Achilleis 1.61-76

Father and Master of the mighty Deep, look, Neptune, at what kind of pitiful use You allow passage across the open seas. Safely under sail pass the crimes of nations, ever since that Pagasean prow ruptured the sanctions of law and the hallowed dignity of the sea while carrying Jason in his quest for plunder. Grant that I may drive off mourning, and that it not be pleasing to You that over so many waves I should find but a single shore to inhabit a sepulcher on some Ilian promontory.

Statius Silvae 3.2.1-49

Gods, who delight in preserving bold ships and turning from them the perils of windy seas, make smooth and placid these waters, and attend with good council my vows, let not my words be drowned out by roaring waves as I pray:

"O Neptune, grand and rare is the pledge we make to You, and in what we commend into the depths of the sea. Young Maecius it is whose body we commit to the sea, far from the sight of land, that he, the better part of our souls, traverses the sea's length and depth (to the Western Lands).

"Bring forth the benign stars, the Spartan brothers, Castor and Pollux, to sit upon the horns of the yard arm. Let your light illuminate sea and sky. Drive off your sister Helen's stormy star, I pray, and expel it from all the heavens.

"And you azure Nereids of the seas, whose good fortune it was to attain mastery of the oceans – may it be allowed to name you stars of the seas – rise up from your glassy caverns near the foaming waves that encircle Doris, and tranquilly swim circles around the shores of Baiae where the hot springs abound. Seek after the lofty ship on which a noble descendant of Ausonians, Celer, mighty at arms, is glad to embark. Not long will you need to look, for she lately came across the sea, leading a convoy laden with Egyptian wheat and bound for Dicarcheis. First was she to salute Capreae and from her starboard side offer a libation of Mareotic wine to

Tyrrhenian Minerva. Near to her, on either side, circle gracefully around her. Divide your labors, some to tighten fast the rigging from masts to deck, while others high above spread forth canvass sails to the westerly Zephyrs. Still others replace some benches, others send into the water the rudder by whose curved blade steers the ship. Another plumbs the depths with leaden weights while others to fasten the skiff that follows astern, and to dive down and drag the hooked anchor from the depths, and one to control the tides and make the sea flow eastward. Let none of the sea green sisterhood be without her task.

"Then let Proteus of manifold shape and triformed Triton swim before, and Glaucus whose loins vanished by sudden enchantment, and who, so oft as he glides up to his native shores, wistfully beats his fish tail on Anthedon's strand.

"But above all others you, Palaemon, with your goddess mother, be favourable, if I have a passion to tell of your own Thebes, and sing of Amphion, bard of Phoebus, with no unworthy quill. "And may the father whose Aeolian prison constrains the winds, whom the various blasts obey, and every air that stirs on the world's seas, and storms and cloudy tempests, keep the North wind and South and East in closer custody behind his wall of mountain, but may Zephyr alone have the freedom of the sky, alone drive vessels onward and skim unceasingly over the crests of billows, until he brings without a storm your glad sails safe to the Paraetonian haven."

Valerius Flaccus Argonautica 1.188-203

"Neptune, Lord of Waters, the highest honor falls to You, along the shoreline, decked with dark blue ribbons, a bull Ancaeus fells, and to Zephyris and Glaucus bulls as well, while a heifer is offered to Thetis. No one is more deft than he with the ritual axe at the fat necks of the cattle. Jason himself pours a goblet in libation to the lord of the sea, saying, "O God, who with a nod can stir the ocean foam, You who with Your salt water encompass the lands of the earth, hear my prayer and grant me Your indulgence. I am the first of mankind to venture forth on unlawful paths across Your waters, and therefore, one might suppose, deserve the worst of Your storms. It is not my own idea to presume in this way, to pile mountain on high mountain and summon down from Olympus bolts of heavenly lightning. Pelias' prayers are false. Do not be swayed by his vows, but know that he devised and imposed his cruel commands to send me off to Colchis and bring on me and my kin the bitterest grief. I beg of You, therefore, mercy and justice. Let Your waters receive me: bear me up and protect this ship and its crew of kings." Thus he spoke as he poured the rich wine from the cup on the blazing coals of fire.

Valerius Flaccus Argonautica 1.667-80

O You Gods who rule the waves and hold domain over the winds and storms, you whose dwelling places reach from the ocean's depths to the heights of heaven, and you Father of the Gods, who order the spheres of the sky and govern the tides, behold a novelty here on earth, a ship on the sea with armed men. For your rage I make atonement and pray you look with indulgence upon us. Let me bring these men safely to shore, and let me go home again where I shall offer up on the sacrificial altars those rich feasts your mercy shall have deserved. In every village and hamlet men shall acknowledge the might of Neptune and pay you homage.

Virgil Aeneid 3.528-9

Gods of land and sea, and of their potent storms, carry us on a gentle breeze and breathe a favorable wind for us to follow.

Virgil Aeneid 5.235-8

Gods, who commands the open seas, upon whose waves I hasten, gladly before your altar on this shore will I arrange the sacrifice of a white bull, this I vow as guarantor, to make his entrails an offering and pour clear wine on the briny sea in your honour.

AE 1997, 977; Hamble, Britannia

Lord Neptune, I commend to You the fellow who pounced upon what rightfully belongs to Muconus and therefore I remit to You the six silver coins along with the one who stole them, whether male or female, whether a boy or a girl, therefore I give to You, Niske, and for Neptune the life, health, and blood of him whose conscious will be filled with guilt, his mind beguiled, he who violated me in here, and who knows his guilt, in order that You ensnare this thief who violate me in this way; may You attack him and consume his blood, Lord Neptune.

Domine Neptune tibi dono hominem qui solidum involavit Muconi et argentiolos sex ideo dono nomina qui decepit si mascel si femina si puer si puella ideo dono tibi Niske et Neptuno vitam valitudinem sanguem eius qui conscius fuerit eius deceptionis animus qui hoc involavit et qui conscius fuerit ut eum decipias furem qui hoc involavit sanguem eius consumas et decipias domine Neptune.

18 PRAYERS TO PATER LIBER

Anomynous Elegy to Maecenus 1.57-68

O Bacchus, after we defeated the dark tanned Indians, You drank sweet wine from Your helmet and, carefree, You loosened Your tunic. It was then I suppose that You dressed in rich purple finery. I am mindful of those times, and certainly recall those snow-white arms shining brightly that led the thyrsus and how You adorned it with gems and gold, and ivy wound thereon as well. Surely silver slippers bound you feet, this, I think, Bacchus, You will not deny. Softer than You usually gave in the many times You counseled me, then was brought forth new words upon Your lips

Caesius Bassius Hymn of Callimachus

Come, O Lyaeus, bihorned Bassareus, two-mothered Maenalius, come into this place I prepare with sleek, shiny hair. May You arouse with a crown of ivy and golden clusters of grapes, and bear shaft of new green wood, O Gentle One, may You come to this altar, Bacchus, Bacchus, Bacchus.

Flores Carmina 2

Bacchus, inventor of vines, may you arrive full of wines, may you pour forth the sweet liquid, to be compared with nectar, and make the old pleasant, and turned to another use, may it not lead harsh flavor to our spiteful veins

Grattius Cynegetica 475-76

Liber expels light cares from the heart, Liber brings soothing relief from distress.

Liber expels pains from the chest, Liber bears medicine to soothe a fever.

Horace Carmina 2.19.7-8

Euhoe! Save me Liber, spare me grave master of the fearful ivy-rod.

Horace Carmina 3.25.19-20

In spring, O Lenaeus Bacchus, I follow You, a god wreathed with ivy.

Nemesianus Eclogue 2.20-24

O Dryades who live in the forest, and Napaeas who live in caves, and Naides whose gleaming white feet pass through waves upon the shore and promote purple violets to grow on grassy slopes, tell me of my Donaces who I came upon under the shadows, in the meadow where she plucked up roses and the shoots of lilies pruned?

Ovid Fasti 3.789-90

Turn Your head with complacent horns to me, Father Bacchus, and give my genius a fair wind to follow

Ovid Metamorphoses 4.11-21; 31

Bacchus they call you, and Bromius, and Lyaeus, born in fire, and Savior also, who alone was born of two mothers. Revered as a God in Nyseus, unshorn Thyoneus, joyful Lenaeus, the sower of grapes, Lord of Nocturnal Revelries, the Bullroarer, and by many more names, Liber, are You known among the Greeks. Adored for your eternal youth, a youth everlasting, you the most beautiful among the celestial Gods high above, to You are sacrifices made when You, without horns upon Your most virgin head, are near and lend us Your assistance. Arising victorious in the East, illuminating those distant lands faded in memory, to outermost India as far as the banks of the Ganges.

Calm and mild, may you come to us.

Ovid Metamorphoses 11.131-32

Forgive me, Father Bacchus, I was mistaken, but have pity, I pray, and command that I should be torn from your beauty.

Propertius Eligiae 3.17.1-20

O Bacchus, humbly now I approach Your altar. Grant tranquil seas for me, Father, and a fair wind in my sails. You are able to tame even the rages of Venus; Your wine a cure for our sorrows. By You are lovers bound to one another; by You are their bonds dissolved. O Bacchus, cleanse my soul of fault.

Truly also You cannot attest to be ignorant of my sorrow when it was your lynxes that carried Ariadne off to the stars, like You there is an old flame still burning in my bones. Only wine or death may rid us of our ills.

Truly an empty night alone and sober spent always torments lovers; where hopes and fears churn in the mind of one or the other. But if, Bacchus, Your gift could soothe my fevered mind and bring sleep to my wearied bones, then I'll plant vines and fasten them in orderly rows upon my hills, and myself stand guard less wild beasts should pluck them.

When my vats fill foaming purple with must, and new wine presses have stained my feet with grapes, then it will be enough for me to live with Your vines and in Your horned presence, O Bacchus, I, Your poet, shall sing.

Statius Thebaid 4.383-404

Almighty Father of Nysa, who long has passed from loving your ancestral rites in distant India, who now is swiftly borne beneath the frozen North to shake warlike Ismara with your thyrsus, you, Bacchus, who now urges the grapevines to overgrow the realm of Lycurgus, or you who is swelling the Ganges and the Red Sea, to the farthest Eastern lands, rushing forward and shouting in triumph, or who from the springs of Hermus rises forth golden, but we, your progeny, have had to lay aside such arms that do you honor at festivals, instead to bear war and tears, alarm and similar horrors, the burdens of unjust reigns. Rather than speak to you once more of the monstrous acts of these leaders and of their vulgar progeny, rather would I have you carry me across the eternally frozen lands beyond the Caucasus Mountains where Amazons howl out their war cries. Behold, you press me hard, Bacchus. Far different from the frenzy I had sworn to you, I saw the clash of two bulls, both alike in honor and sharing one lineage, butting heads and locking their horns in fierce combat and both perish in their shared wrath. You are the worse evil. You depart. Guilty are you who pray that he alone should gain possession of ancestral pastures and hills whose ownership is shared with others. Evil one, born of the wretched, so much has warfare and bloodshed brought you; now another leader holds your glades and pastures.

Sulpicia 4.5.9

Grant, O natal Genius, all my heart's desires, and expensive incense I shall burn upon your altar.

Tibullus 2.1.3-4; 17-20

Come to us, Bacchus, with clusters of grapes dangling from your horns, and you, too, Ceres, a wreath of newly ripened wheat for your temples, come!

Gods of our fathers, we purify our farmers and our fruitful fields; we ask that you drive away harm from our borders. Let not the now sprouting plants succumb before harvest, let not the timid lambs be outrun by swift wolves.

Tibullus 3.6.1-4

Splendid Liber, draw near to me! With your forever mystical vine, and your ivy bound head, carry off my sorrows, in the same manner as you have so often used wine's healing powers to overcome the pangs of love.

Virgil Georgics 2.2-8

Now shall I sing of you, Bacchus. Without you there would be no woodland or thicket, or slow growing olive grove. Come hither, O Lenaean Father, all things here beckon to be nurtured by your many gifts, the autumn vineshoots laden the countryside with blossoms, the vintage grape harvest foams plentiful to the lips of the wine vats. Hasten, O Lenaean Father, come and, stripped down, tinge your naked feet in new wine must with me.

19 PRAYERS TO TELLUS

Antonius Musa Precatio Terrae

Holy Goddess, Tellus, Mother of all Nature, engendering all things and regenerating them each day, as You alone bring forth from Your womb all things into life.

Heavenly Goddess, overseeing all things on earth and throughout the seas, in whatever by silent nature is restored in sleep and in death, in the same way that You put to flight the Night with the Light You restore each day.

Earth, Enricher of Life, You dispel the dark shadow of death and the disorder of vast endless Chaos. You hold back the winds and storms, the rain showers and tempests. You alone regulate the weather cycles, either bestirring or putting to flight the storm, interspersing them with cheerful days.

You give the Food of Life unfailingly, in fidelity, and when the soul by necessity departs, in You alone do we find refuge. Thus, whatever You give, in You all will be returned. Deservedly are You called Great Mother of the Gods. Piously then are all the celestial powers distilled in You. The One and True parent of all living things, human and divine. Without You nothing could be born, nothing could grow, and nothing mature.

You are the Great Goddess, the Queen of Heaven, You, Goddess, I adore. I call upon Your power, come. Make what I ask to be readily and easily accomplished, and draw my thanks, Mother Earth, that, in fidelity, You do rightly merit

Hear me, please, and favor me. This I ask of You, Holy Mother, and may You willingly give answer to me: May whatever herbs grow by Your providence bring health to all humankind. May You now send these forth to me as Your medicines. May they be filled with Your healing virtues. May everything that I prepare from these herbs have good result, each and every one in the same way. As I shall receive these herbs from You, so too shall I willingly give them out to others, so that their health too may be ensured through Your good graces. Finally, Mother Earth, ensure Your healing powers for me as well. This I humbly ask.

Corpus Inscriptiones Latinae VI 32323, Acta Sacrorum Saecularium, Rome, Lines 136-37; ref. L. 92-99

Terra Mater, as it is prescribed for you in those books –and for this reason may every good fortune attend the Roman people, the Quirites – let sacrifice be made to you with a pregnant sow of your own, as a whole burnt offering. I beg and pray [that you may increase the sovereign power and majesty of the Roman people, the Quirites, in war and peace; as you have always watched over us among the Latins. Forever may you grant safety, victory and health to the Roman people, the Quirites. May you bestow your favor on the Roman people, the Quirites, and on the legions of the Roman people, the Quirites. May you preserve the health and welfare of the people of Rome, the Quirites, and may you always remain willingly favorable and propitious to the people of Rome, the Quirites, to the college of the quindecimviri, to me, to my house and household. May you accept [this] sacrifice of (a pregnant sow), to be burnt whole for you in sacrifice. For these reasons may you be honored and strengthened with the sacrifice of this (pregnant sow), and become favorable and propitious to the Roman people, the

Quirites, to the college of the quindecimviri, to myself, to my house, and to my household.]

Julian the Blessed IV.112

Who is the Mother of the Gods? She is the source of the intellectual and creative gods, who, in their turn guide the visible gods: She is both the Mother and Spouse of mighty Jupiter; She came into being next to and together with the great creator; She is in control of every form of life, and the cause of all generation; She easily brings to perfection all things that are made, without pain She brings to birth, and with the Father's aid creates all things that are; She is the motherless maiden, enthroned at the side of Jupiter, and in very truth is the Mother of All the Gods. For having received into Herself the causes of all the gods, both intelligible and supramundane, She became the source of the intellectual gods.

Statius Thebiad 8.303-38

O eternal Creatrix of Gods and men, who animates forest and stream with soul, and joins seeds of life together throughout the world, and You bear the stones of Pyrrha that were enlivened into men by the hand of Prometheus. Hungry men You were first to give nourishment with a variety of foods. You encircle and carry the sea within You. Under Your power are the gentleness of domesticated herds and the ferocity of wild beasts and the repose from flight of birds. Firm and immobile, unsetting power of the earth suspended in the vacuum of space, You are the center around which the rapid heavens revolve. All the heavenly bodies, in chariots of fire, wheel about You, O center of the universe, indivisible from the Great Brotherhood of the Gods. Therefore are You the Bountiful who nourishes so many nations, and at the same time so many high cities and so many noble peoples. You provide Yourself and all the world as one, from above and below. You carry without effort to Yourself Atlas, who toils to hold up the celestial field of stars. We alone do You refuse to carry. Do we weigh You down, Goddess? For what unwitting wrong, I pray, must we atone? That we would so soon come here as a small band of strangers from distant Inachian shores? It is unworthy of You, most beneficial Goddess, to set limits by such cruel means on every side against all that is human merely by birth, against people who everywhere are Your own. May You then abide with and bear arms for all alike. I pray You allow that those warriors who spend their last breathe in the battle will have their souls return once more into the heavens. Do not so suddenly carry us off to our tomb and take the breath from our body. Do not be in such haste; soon enough we will come as all do when You lead them along the path that all must travel. Only listen to our pleas and keep a level plain for the Pelasgians and do not hasten the swift Fates. And You, dear to the Gods, not by any hand or Sidonian sword were you dispatched, but mighty Nature opened Her heart to you, entombing you for your merits in Cirrha's chasm, welcoming you in Her loving embrace. May You joyously grant, I pray, that I may come to know You in my prayers, that You may council me on the heavens and give true warnings from Your prophetic altars, and that You may teach me what You are prepared to reveal to people. I will perform Your rites of divination, and in Apollo's absence I will call Your prophet and upon Your divine spirit for visions. That distant place to which You hurry is, to me, more potent than all the shrines of Delos and Cirrha, better by far than the sanctuary of any other shrine.

Virgil Aeneid 7.120

Hail, O Mother Tellus, for whom I am destined, and you, too, faithful Gods of Troy, hail O Penates. This is our home; this, our homeland.

20 PRAYERS TO VENUS

Anthologia Latina I 781.15

Grant, I pray, your assistance and ease the pain of our fiery passions.

Apuleius Metamorphoses 11.2

O blessed Queen of Heaven, celestial Venus, who in the beginning of the world did join all kinds of things with an engendered love, by an eternal propagation of life, now worshipped within the Temple of the Isle of Paphos; You who is worshipped in divers manners, and does illuminate all the borders of the earth by Your feminine shape, You which nourishes all the fruits of the world by Your vigor and force; with whatsoever name or fashion it is lawful to call upon You, I pray You end my great travail and misery, and deliver me from the wretched fortune, which has for so long a time pursued me. Grant peace and rest if it please You to reply to my entreaties, for I have endured too much labor and peril.

Horcae Carmina 1.30.1-8

Come to us Venus, O Queen of Cnidos and Paphos, leave Cyprus, though the isle is dear to You, come instead to where the incense is thick and Glycera sings to You, that you may transfer Your home to a new shrine among us. Bring along for Your company desirous Cupid, loose- girdled Graces and Nymphs, youthful Juventus and Mercury, who without You are graceless.

Horcae Carmina 4.1.1-2

After so long a time, do You once more disturb my peace of mind with desires? Spare me, Venus, I pray, I beg of You!

Laevius FPR fr. 26

Therefore adoring You as though You were nurturing Venus Herself, whether You are female, or whether You are male, even so, Illuminating the Night, You are a nurturing Moon.

Lucretius De Rerum Natura 1.1-9

Venus Genetrix, charmer of gods and mankind, nurturing Mother, beneath the starry signs that glide through the night, You enliven the ship-bearing seas and the fruitful earth, since it is through You that all things are conceived and animated into life to behold the Light of Day. Goddess, for You the winds make way, the heavenly clouds open at Your coming, the miraculous earth greets You with sweet scented flowers, for You the surface of the seas laugh, and the peaceful heavens glisten in luminescence.

Martial Epigrammata 9.90.13-18

Restore our youth, Venus, restore our healthy glow, and the kalends of March they will devote to the Paphian goddess. Gladly will the procession wind to Your altar, in shining white robes they will bring You sweet incense and pure wine, served with glistening morsels of meat piled as delicate petit fors.

Nemesianus Eclogue 2.57-59

Venus, Daughter of Dione, You who touches the lofty ridges of Eryx, into whose care, throughout all the centuries, the unions of men and their lovers have been placed, what, I pray, have I come to merit?

Ovid Ars Amore 1.30

Restore our youth, Venus, restore our healthy glow, and the kalends of March they will devote to the Paphian goddess. Gladly will the procession wind to Your altar, in shining white robes they will bring You sweet incense and pure wine, served with glistening morsels of meat piled as delicate petit fors.

Ovid Ars Amore 2.14-15

Now, if ever before, I required Your favor, Venus Cytherrea, and that of Your son, and now, too, Erato, whose erotic name exudes Love.

Ovid Amores 1.3.1-6

My prayer is just. May Venus hear all our many prayers. Take one who would serve You through long years, accept one who knows how to love with a pure heart.

Ovid Amores 3.2.55-7

Winsome Venus, to You we pray, and to Your children with the mighty bow Assent to my undertaking, and may You change my lady's mind, make her open to love.

Ovid Heroides 15.57-58

I am Yours, Venus Ericina, who also celebrates the Sicilian mountains, O Goddess, look after your prophetic poet, you who has the name of Love.

Ovid Fasti 4.1

Nurturing Venus, Mother of the twin Loves, favour me.

Ovid Metamorphoses 10.640-41

Venus of Cytherea, I pray that you come to our venture, and that she gives herself to whom you help in passion.

Petronius Arbiter Satyricon 85

Dear Venus, if I may kiss this boy without his knowing, a pair of doves I'll give tomorrow.

Plautus Bacchides 892-95

By Jupiter and all the gods and goddesses, Juno and Ceres, Minerva, Latona, Hope, and Ops, Virtue, Venus, Castor and Pollux, Mars, Mercurius, Hercules, Summanus, Sol and Saturnus, I swear she is not lying with him, walking hand-in-hand with him, kissing him full upon the lips, or in any other way, as they say, being familiar with him.

Plautus Miles Gloriosus 1228-30

Venus, I offer You thanks, and I beg and entreat You that I may win the man I love and long for, and that he may be gracious to me, and not reject my desire for him.

Plautus Poenulus 125

Venus, of the little I have to offer, I willingly give You a little.

Plautus Rodens 694-701

Kind Venus, tearfully we plead to You, as we kneel and clasp this your altar, receive us into Your safekeeping and watch over us. Take vengeance on the wicked who have belittled your sanctuary, and in Your goodness let us remain at this altar as a refuge from our suffering... be not offended with us, nor hold us at fault, if there be anything about us that to you is unclean.

Plautus Rodens 702-5

Venus, I think that this is a fair request and that you should grant it. Their fears have driven them to it. If you yourself, as they say, came from a seashell, then you should not object to the soiled shell of their garments.

Plautus Rudens 144-46

May Venus, or better still Ceres see that no risk of danger befall you as you travel from here to your home for lunch; Venus cares for lovers, Ceres cares for wheat.

Plautus Rudens 1348-9

Venus, I pray to You that all pimps may suffer.

Propertius Eligiae 2.16.13-14

O Venus, come quickly now to give succor to our sorrows; may love erupt in the hearts of those passionate limbs we continually desire.

Propertius Eligiae 3.4.19-22

Preserve one of Your own sons, Venus, let it be in this lifetime, may You perceive those remaining descendents of Aeneas. May there be plunder enough in this for them, that honest rewards are piled up from hard work. For me it shall be enough if able to dance along the Sacred Way in praise of the Gods.

Statius Achilleis 1.143-44

Lead on, O best of Mothers, I plead, lead on, and exhaust the Gods with humble entreaties (on my behalf).

Tibullus 1.2.41-2; 56; 99-100

"Venus born of blood and thought to be born of the ocean, too."

Three times sing, (I'm told), and three times spit upon the ground as you say this charm.

"At the very least, Venus, preserve one who in his heart always serves you. What offerings shall I set upon your altar to appease your anger?"

Tibullus 3.3.33-8

Come, Saturn's daughter, give favor to my prayer! Hear me, Cyprian Venus, who was born along on a conch shell! Rather let my fate be denied, than that my life should now be sorrowfully ended by those sisters who spin the threads of everyone's future, and called down by ghastly Orcus into the desolate swamps and sluggish streams of black waters.

Tibullus 3.9.4

May Venus keep him safe for me; may Amor preserve my love.

Valerius Flaccus Argonautica 2.611-12

O Cretheian Virgin, borne on graceful and gentle waves, unfold the way, Goddess, and show us what course to follow.

Virgil Catalepton 14

If I am to further my undertaking, to traverse all the world, O Venus, who dwells in Paphos and in Idalian groves, so that Trojan Aeneas is thought worthy at last to sail with You in song through Roman towns, not only with incense or painted tablet shall I adorn Your temple, and with pure hands bring You garlands, but a humble offering of a horned ram and a bull, the greatest sacrifice, their blood a priest shall sprinkle into the fire of an altar erected in Your honor, and a marble painted in a thousand colours for You, a picture of Amor with His quiver. Come, O Goddess of Cythera, Your own Caesar and an altar along Sorrento's shore beckon You from Olympus.

21 PRAYERS TO VESTA

Cicero De Domo sua ad Pontifices 144-5

Mother Vesta, I pray to You, whose most chaste Vestales I have defended against pillage and desecration by demented men; for their eternal flame I could not allow to pass, extinguished in the blood of citizens, or Your pure flame be intermingled with a conflagration sweeping the entire city.

I call You as witness, I place myself and my family in Your hands, in these struggles I devoted myself and my life, while consul and before, without regard for my own interests, or for profit, but strove in all my actions and thoughts with vigilance for the safety and health of all my fellow citizens, then, that someday I might bid to enjoy seeing the Republic restored at last. But if my counsel had not benefited my country, then in perpetual misery would I suffer, departed from my family, friends and all sustenance. When by Your favor my home is restored to me, may I at long last be allowed to consider it demonstrated that this devotion of my life has met with the approval of the Gods.

Ovid Fast 3.426-28

Vesta, watch over him whose hand tends the Holy Fire. Live well, fires. O live, I pray, undying flames.

Ovid Fasti 4.827-32

Then king Romulus said, "As I found this city, be present, Jupiter, Father Mars, and Mother Vesta, and all gods who it is pious to summon, join together to attend. Grant that my work may rise with Your auspices. Grant that it may for many years hold dominion on earth, and assert its power over the east and west.

Ovid Fasti 6.249-50

Vesta favor me. To You now our voices lift in praise as by this rite it is allowed that we may approach You.

Valerius Maximus 8.1.5 (absol.)

(Vestal Virgin Tuccia prayed for proof of her innocence:) O Vesta, if I have always brought pure hands to your secret services, make it so now that with this sieve I shall be able to draw water from the Tiber and bring it to Your temple.

Vellius Paterculus II 131.1

Jupiter Capitolinus, Mars Gradivus called progenitor and aide of the Romans, Vesta, perpetual guardian of fire, and whatever divine powers in this greatness of Roman sovereignty, the largest empire on earth, exulted to the highest dignity, to You the public voice calls to witness and to pray: guard, preserve, and protect this state, this peace, this prince, and those who succeed to the Senate, by their long standing, determined worthy to consider the most grave matters among mortals.

22 PRAYERS TO VULCANUS

Grattius Faliscus Gynegetica 437-42

Holy Vulcanus, foremost of those who cherish this place, to You we pray for peace. Grant Your ultimate assistance to the tired and worn, and, if no one here merits punishment for some noxious crime, may You have mercy on all their souls and allow them to reach Your purifying fountains. Three times they invoke Your name, three times they pour rich incense upon the focal fire, and strew the altar with auspicious boughs in Your honor.

Martial Epigrammata 5.7.5 To Vulcan

Soon, I pray, Vulcan, memories of whispered rumors of disgrace and loud quarrels of complaint You will no longer hold against the children of Mars; we are also the children of Your sweet wife Venus, spare us, Father.

23 PRAYERS I HAVE WRITTEN

LVCIVS VITELLIVS TRIARIVS

Prayer to_____ Date_____

For_____

MEDITATIONS ON THE ROMAN DEITIES

Prayer to_____ Date_____

For_____

Prayer to_____ Date_____

For_____

Prayer to_____ Date_____

For_____

Prayer to_____ Date_____

For_____

MEDITATIONS ON THE ROMAN DEITIES

Prayer to_____ Date_____

For_____

Prayer to_____ Date_____

For_____

_____

_____

_____

_____

_____

_____

_____

_____

_____

_____

_____

_____

Prayer to_____ Date_____

For_____

Prayer to_____ Date_____

For_____

_____

_____

_____

_____

_____

_____

_____

_____

_____

_____

_____

_____

Prayer to _____ Date _____

For _____

Prayer to_____ Date_____

For_____

MEDITATIONS ON THE ROMAN DEITIES

Prayer to_____ Date_____

For_____

Prayer to_____ Date_____

For_____

MEDITATIONS ON THE ROMAN DEITIES

Prayer to_____ Date_____

For_____

Prayer to_____ Date_____

For_____

MEDITATIONS ON THE ROMAN DEITIES

Prayer to_____ Date_____

For_____

Prayer to_____ Date_____

For_____

MEDITATIONS ON THE ROMAN DEITIES

Prayer to _____ Date _____

For _____

Prayer to_____ Date_____

For_____

_____

_____

_____

_____

_____

_____

_____

_____

_____

_____

_____

Prayer to_____ Date_____

For_____

Prayer to_____ Date_____

For_____

_____

_____

_____

_____

_____

_____

_____

_____

_____

_____

_____

_____

Prayer to_____ Date_____

For_____

Prayer to_____ Date_____

For_____

Prayer to_____ Date_____

For_____

Prayer to_____ Date_____

For_____

_____

_____

_____

_____

_____

_____

_____

_____

_____

_____

_____

_____

_____

MEDITATIONS ON THE ROMAN DEITIES

Prayer to _____ Date _____

For _____

_____

_____

_____

_____

_____

_____

_____

_____

_____

_____

_____

_____

_____

Prayer to_____ Date_____

For_____

ABOUT THE AUTHOR

Lucius Vitellius Triarius, aka Chip Hatcher, is a Graduate (cum Laude) in Political Science, focusing in Ancient Mediterranean Political Systems, from the University of Tennessee at Knoxville and resides in the foothills of the Great Smoky Mountains in Eastern Tennessee.

He is also a member of Nova Roma (www.novaroma.org), a global Roman Reconstruction project, advocating the via Romana, or Roman Way, where he serves as a Provincial Governor and Senator of Nova Roma.

The Roman Way is the study and practical application of "Romanitas" and the "mos maiorum", the revival of all aspects of Roman life, culture, virtues, ethics and philosophies in our everyday lives.

It is as part of the mos maiorum that citizens are expected to take up Roman names for use within the society. Learning Latin, the language of Roman culture, is also an equally important step towards becoming a modern Roman.

One of the cornerstones of Romanitas are the Roman virtues; those qualities which define the ideal state of being and behavior of the Roman citizen.

He believes that we must remember and preserve the good parts of the past in the present, so that others will remember it in the future.

f·i·n·i·s

Printed in Great Britain
by Amazon